The Angora Chronicles

Musings of an Old Goat

Volume One

Ronnie Lewis

Ronnie Lewis

Library of Congress-Cataloged-in-Publication Data

Copyright © 2014 Ronnie Lewis
all rights reserved.
ISBN-13: 978-1505289398
ISBN-10: 1505289394

DEDICATIONS

TO THE MEMORY OF MY PARENTS
CECIL AND BONNIE GAY

MY FRIENDS: PAST, PRESENT, FUTURE,

MY BROTHER KENNY

AND ESPECIALLY TO MADELINE
AND OUR FAMILY

~~~~~~~~~~~

TABLE OF CONTENTS

A LAST WORD FROM THE AUTHOR

THE CHRONICLES

I really took to the name *The Angora Chronicles* when my friend and school classmate Grant Ray Thompson suggested it because angora goats were mine and my Brother Kenny's first business venture.

The year was 1960. Shelton Kennedy (one of my Dads very best friends) was a goat man. When it came time to sell off his years kid crop, he sold 20 freshly weaned goats to each of us for $2 each. We had no money so he let us pay him after they were sheared and we had collected the money.

We lived on 65 acres of the hilliest... rockiest pasture land in all of central Texas. It was at the top end of a Bull Creek Tributary south of Jollyville a few miles. The place was covered with Shin Oak Brush, a favorite diet of goats. So we didn't have to buy feed.

In just a couple of months we sheared them for the first time. The yield was 3-4 lbs each and fine kid hair fetched the best price, around $1.50 per lb. By the time we paid the shearing crew $.50 per head to shear, we ended up with the goats paid for and money in our pockets. We sheared twice each year and they soon started making babies. It turned out to be a fine enterprise for a couple of kids.

The other component to my love of goats was, that from the time I was 12, and Kenny a couple of years older, we hired out to help several ranchers around Smithwick gather goats at shearing time. The job included riding horses', getting up and in the pens, sorting, drenching, doing unmentionables to the young males and then helping haul and tromp down the mohair in huge sacks so that the most hair could be stuffed into each sack.

There were two shearing as I mentioned earlier... in February when it was the coldest, and the first part of September when it was hot. The dust created with that operation was unbelievable. It made you appreciate getting home and taking a bath. We made $8 - $10 per day for our service.

Last year I was honored to attend Shelton Kennedy's 90 birthday party. Besides Shelton, others we helped with goats were Cecil Lewis, Jim

Layton Cox, Melvin Heine, Landis Wier, and Loftin Meredith. They have all left us now, as has the market for mohair. But my fond memories live on.

So welcome to The Angora Chronicles and the Musings of an Old Goat.

~~~~~~~~~~

~~~~~~~~~~

The Sound of Hoof-Beats

I was the kind of kid who wanted to ride a donkey even if everyone else rode horses. Tar Baby was an average little donkey to most but he was my pride and joy. We were in rodeo parades together with me dressed as a clown. Kenny, my older brother, was quite the horseman. He lived to break and train horses. I was made to help with the horse breaking, but it was something that I could have done without.

By the time I was 7 or 8 years old our spending money came from working with Shetland Ponies. Like I said we lived on the rockiest 65 acres on the face of the earth, and being thrown off was not ever something you wanted to do. We had as many as twelve to fifteen horses that we were breaking at any one time. At $35 each to ride these little guys we were making some good money for the late 50's & early 60's.

Kenny, being two and a half years older and bigger, always came out on top of any disagreement between us. Two of his favorite methods of entertainment were at my expense. The first was roping me on foot with him on horseback and trotting off just fast enough that if I ran at full speed I could keep up. At least for a while, then I would always tire out before his horse and him. It was always my fault when I ended up skinned from head to toe.

His other favorite past time was riding up behind me with him on a full sized horse while I rode a Shetland or Tar Baby. As he approached he would leap out of the saddle and ride me all the way to the ground. That usually left me skinned and bruised worse than towing me with the rope. His landing was always pretty good as I was the cushion between him and the hard ground.

On that one day when I heard the hoof beats

behind me I knew what I was in for. Luckily I was on Prince a very good handling little Shetland. Kenny was coming up on my left side. My timing could not have been better, as he left his saddle I pulled back and hard to the right. He plowed up more gravel and rocks than I ever had.

What sweet revenge. I couldn't help it, I laughed until I almost fell off the pony. I don't think I ever saw Kenny so mad. He got even madder when I rode off without catching his horse and he had to walk about a mile to get home. I don't remember ever hearing those hoof beats coming up behind me the same way again.

~~~~~~~~~~~~

Dove Hunting Story

People who know me today, the big lug I am, don't realize how incredibly small I was at least until I reached the 11th grade. I was a midget, and then grew a foot in my last two years of high school. When you grow up in rugged circumstances and you are small you have to watch your every move. Someone is out to pick on you at every turn.

A few days ago an old friend Terry Becker from Marble Falls came to visit me here in Corpus Christi. His son and family were with him as well as my nephew and his family. Terry reminded me of a dove hunting escapade at one of our stock tanks at Smithwick.

About a dozen of my brother's friends were there, all being either a year or two years older than me. When they'd shot up all their shells, they sent me to the opposite side of stock tank to fetch more. As soon as I was at a safe distance, (their claims not mine,) they started peppering me with bird shot. I was truly far enough away that if a pellet hit me it wouldn't penetrate even if it did sting.

Determined to not let them have the best of me, I kept walking toward the pickup where there was a 22 caliber semi-automatic rifle; a great rabbit gun. I drew it out and began firing hitting the ground right below them. They were running, trying to hide behind bushes, behind each other. There really wasn't any place for them to hide. After I'd emptied the clip we decided on our own brand of a cease-fire.

At the time I was sure that the lead was just going into the ground. Only years later did I realize just how much those bullets will ricochet. But it had an impact on all the big boys I suppose. One of them still remembered it fifty years later. Thanks for that memory, Terry Becker.

~~~~~~~~~~

My First Day to Attend
School in Marble Falls

I went to school in a small three room schoolhouse at Jollyville for my first 7 years. Starting the 8th grade in Marble Falls was the first and only time I ever switched schools. I had it pretty good over a lot of kids moving to a new school because I already knew a lot of the kids there. I had been around MF nearly every weekend and summer for my whole life. Running around with Glenn Lewis gave me the chance to meet a bunch of people and be exposed to a lot of situations.

Jimmy Frasier was the one person I probably knew best. When we made it to science class that first day the desks were arranged in alphabetical order to where Jimmy was across the aisle from me. Another new boy, Holland Lester, was directly in front of me. That year the school officials had decided that separating the boys and girls was the best way to keep order. Jimmy, being the agitator he was, kept on goading me to jab Holland in the back with a sharp pencil. I suppose with me wanting to fit in I was happy to cause a little confusion.

After I did it a couple of times and him jumping with each poke Holland finally had enough and jump-ed up ready to attack me. The teacher, Lanny Thompson (or was it Lannie), not wanting to let things get out of hand on the first day called Holland to the front. He said he wasn't going to allow that kind of conduct in his class and bent Holland over and swatted him three little licks with his wooden paddle. Jimmy and I both were laughing because the new kid got licks the first day.

When Holland returned to his seat the teacher said, "Mr. Frasier and Mr. Lewis, come up here." He then showed the two of us ten each of the hardest licks you could even imagine. He had been paying better attention to our actions than we realized. From that day on we all knew that if we got out of line, it was going to hurt.

~~~~~~~~~~~

The Teacher's Pet

I wasn't the most well behaved student in Mrs. Corker's 8th grade class, but because I had just changed schools I must have tried hard to fit in. I certainly got my share of attention for a new kid.

She was considered a good teacher, but very stern. English was my most difficult subject. Didn't like it, didn't understand it. Mrs. Corker didn't take to students that failed to excel in English. It was obvious that the two of us were going nowhere fast. One day during class, she was talking about baking pies and cookies and such. It seemed that she was hinting that she could use some nice pecans. This was my chance. We had a lot of pecans. That night I shelled a Kerr quart jar full of perfect halves. It took a while, but the next morning might just have been the only day that I was anxious to go to school.

On the bus headed for school I had those beautiful pecans sitting on the seat next to me. A couple of miles from school the bus driver could see a car in the center of the upcoming bridge. It was a narrow bridge. Irby, the bus driver, slammed on the brakes to avoid tangling with the car. The only crash that happened that day was my Kerr jar of pecans hitting the floor.

The thought, "Should I pick up the pecans and put them in my pockets...?" ran through my mind. I had plenty of pockets. "But what would I do after I got to school...?" Before I knew it, the problem was solved. One hundred small feet had taken care of everything. Had it not been for that car on the bridge I could have become Mrs. Corkers' favorite student at least for the day.

~~~~~~~~~~

Jake the Building Trades Teacher

I always considered Jake pretty easy going, know-
ledgeable and a good teacher. But if you got him
riled up, you better watch out. Some of the older
guys and a few of the younger ones were real
hoodlums. They would always try Jake on for size,
and he swung a hard paddle.

The maddest I ever saw that man was pretty late
in the school year. A couple of young little pretties
were dispatched from the school newspaper to do a
story on the Building Trades Program. Jake had told
us they were coming and we needed to be on our best
behavior. All was going great as I remember until one
of them asked if any of us had suggestions for making the next year even better. My hand went up in
the air and I said I just knew of one thing: "I think
if they let girls come down to ENTER the COURSE it
would be better." I went lightly on the first part
but accentuated the other two words. Jake was
sitting there getting more red-faced by the second.
He was chewing on his old pipe and you would have
thought he was going to bite the end of it off.

With the girls gone he let it be known how upset
he was that I had shown disrespect to those young
ladies. He said he wasn't even sure he wanted to
teach a class of boys like us. Then he brought me to

the front, bent me over and went to work on my backside. That may have been when I decided corporal punishment should be outlawed. Even though the whole class tried to explain what was actually said, he was having no part of it.

~~~~~~~~~~

Left To Sweat It Out

I was a sophomore in high school and still small for my age. All the big boys still liked to pick on me, but I'm sure I provoked a lot of it. It was in the building trades program that we learned about carpentry and actually built a house during the school year. Our teacher was Robert Woodard, but like I said we called him Jake. Our shop classroom was in the old bus barn. It was just a big tin building with no insulation. The temperatures in that building could be extreme.

We were a rowdy class and had caused enough trouble that the school board was considering abandoning the program at midterm that year. Everyone knew that if we didn't change our ways, we would be back in a classroom all afternoon rather than outside actually learning something. Jake did everything he and his wooden paddle could do to keep us in line. But we were really a bunch of misfits.

A new high school was being built and would be ready for us to move in at midterm. The new desks to furnish the rooms had arrived and with no other place to store them they brought the dozens of boxes to the bus barn. The boxes were stacked four high, almost to the ceiling.

One day, with the days still very hot, we were loading the bus with tools to go to the house to work. Several of the older classmates decided they would bind my hands and feet, and then put me on top of the boxes. As I struggled to free myself I heard the bus leaving. A few minutes later the School Superintendent, Mr. Wann, came by to inventory the boxes. I had just gained my freedom but was still on top of the boxes. Mr. Wann walked around that stack of boxes time after time with a clipboard in hand. He was no more than four or five feet from me at times.

It was so hot laying up there I could feel sweat pouring off me. My eyes followed him as far as possible with each trip he made around the boxes. Then I would quietly roll over as I heard him coming down the other side. I couldn't make any sudden moves. How would I explain being left behind?

He was there for probably no more than ten minutes, but it felt like hours. To my relief I finally heard the door open then slam shut. He was gone. I climbed down and found something to do while I waited for the bus to return.

Finally I heard the bus pull up. I figured that if I stood back and waited for the others to come in I could just mix in and Jake would never realize I had not been with them all afternoon. As he walked through the door he hollered my name. As I stepped forward he said, "Lewis bend over that'll cost you ten licks."

~~~~~~~~~~

Hay Hauling – Smithwick Style

At 15 cents per bale three young boys could make a fortune hauling hay, or so we thought. Our Dad furnished the pickup, a 55 Chevy $\frac{3}{4}$ ton with a 4 speed and a 6 cylinder engine. But we had to pay for gas, which was cheap - $.30 per gal, and flat repairs, which were a big unknown. We kept several spare tires around just in case. That's what you did back in those days.

Kenny was the driver, the pusher, the big boss man of the bunch. That left Big Jimmy Palmer and me to load the hay out in the fields. We, or rather the Big Boss Man, decided we could each make 3 cents for the work and he, Kenny, would use the left over 6 cents to buy gas and fix flats. The two peons' didn't really get a vote. That was just the way it was going to be.

Big Boss Man also decided it would be fair if we could alternate jobs. For half the time Jimmy would be out throwing the hay up to me to stack. We would then alternate. The only one not alternating was Kenny. He found it necessary to always drive. Once again, that was the way it was going to be.

We could stack 45 bales on each load and depending on the distance we could make a trip per hour. If we stayed after it Jimmy and I would make between $10 and $15 a day. We felt pretty good about that until we figured out Kenny was getting 3 times as much as each of us. Gas was only costing $6 or $8 per day. Even fixing flats didn't cost but a dollar or so each.

The hotter we got out in the summer heat, the more taken advantage of Jimmy and I felt. When we felt like we couldn't go another inch, I'd wait until we were close to a shade tree along the edge of the field, or in our big field at the lake where there was a nice shady pecan out in middle, then at the right time I would stick my hay hook under a rear tire. When we could hear the air coming out one of us would holler, "Sounds like we are having another flat!" Kenny would pull over, get out and set to work changing the tire as we sat in the shade and watched. He didn't dare ask us to help for fear we would be entitled to part of the 'extra' money.

Something tells me we all three ended up making about the same when everything was all tallied up. Funny how those things have a way of working out.

~~~~~~~~~~

The Gift

One of my best memories growing up was that hard work of hauling hay. A couple of years ago when Madeline and I turned 60, our kids with Kenny and Carol threw us a grand party out at Kenny's place on Cow Creek. Jimmy Palmer brought me one of the best gifts I could have received. It was his hay hook that had hung in their barn for all these years.

He wanted me to have it to remind me of the time he jumped out to open a gate and when he got back in I had positioned his hay hook so that he plopped his big butt down in it. It violated him pretty good (or would that be pretty bad.) The old, "bled like a stuck hog," saying came to life that day.

We usually enjoyed doing things to each other, but I remember kinda feeling sorry for Jimmy at least for a few minutes. If you notice, for some reason we always thought that sharpening our hooks to a point was cool. They really didn't need to be that sharp. Anyway, I'll always cherish this gift.

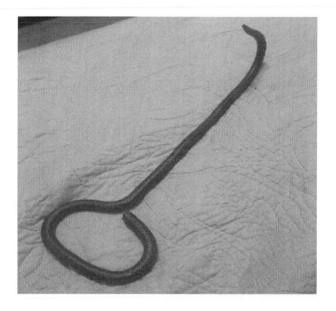

~~~~~~~~~~

The Big Lizard

When I was a kid growing up in Jollyville a family named Travis moved in. They had a boy Kenny's age, a boy my age, and a set of twins who were younger. We lived on 65 acers of a rocky-ledgy-snake-infested-hillside with lots of rattlesnakes and even more copperheads. When the Travis boys came over to our place they were more than happy to pick up and handle any snake we came across. Kenny and I both thought those boys were out of their minds. He and I were hunting the biggest rocks we could find and still be able to pick up and throw at them, from a safe distance.

Anyway when we went to their house they kept all kinds of reptiles. The little twins rode this one big lizard around in the yard. I'm not kidding you. They would climb up on it and ride it around the yard. One day the big lizard came up missing. I think maybe the kids were riding it and forgot to close the door on its cage.

The little old house we lived in was very small and Kenny and I slept on a fold down couch that momma made down every night. But somewhere along the way our Grandma Nancy bought a small mobile home (trailer house to us back then) and parked it a little ways out from our place. When she would go off to visit another of her children (she had 11 kids so there was a lot of visiting) Kenny and I made her place ours. The only problem was we never had a working flashlight. So to get to our bed we would run as fast as we could in the dark to the trailer so snakes wouldn't bite us; or that was our theory. Then the lizard got loose and our anxiety levels increased tenfold. We were sure it was going to grab us as we ran across the rocky expanse to the door. We would go one at a time so it couldn't get us both.

When the lizard didn't get us on the way there it was because it has gotten inside the trailer house during the day and was going to crawl out from under the bed. When that didn't happen, we'd lay there hearing it bump under the floor and make scratching noises until we'd finally go to sleep.

After missing for several months the lizard was found over by Georgetown somewhere; the opposite direction from our house. I'm not completely sure, but I think that it never fully recovered and died not long after it was found.

I'm sure this sounds like a tall tale. Why would people have a lizard and let their kids ride it? Who were these kids that played with snakes? This family operated the Snake Farm that most of us have driven by all our lives on I-35 in New Braunfels, Texas.

They had another operation up in Pennsylvania I think it was.

If anyone cares to check out the validity of this story; the next time you get your bugs sprayed by Travis Pest Control there in Marble Falls or see the owner around town, just ask him. That will be Wayne Travis the boy who was my age.

~~~~~~~~~~~

My Thumbs

When we were kids, well teenagers, Cec had Kenny and me constructing a new shop building out from the house in Smithwick. It was a pipe frame, a simple structure. The cross bracings were used sucker rods ... the steel rod lengths that were used with wind-mills to connect the wind-motor to the bottom pump.

It was a misty rainy day. Kenny, using the skills he had learned in Ag Class, was doing the welding. My job was to hold the long lengths of sucker rod. With it being wet, when he would strike an arc I could feel the current flow through my body. In normal fashion Kenny would lash out at me if I didn't hold the piece steady. I didn't exactly enjoy the jolt I was getting each time he started welding but I endured. I finally figured out that if I'd put the bar in place then press hard on it with my thumbs I would only feel the shock right at the point of contact. After a few hours we were finished with that phase of the job.

About two days later I woke up with both of my thumbs swollen to nearly four times their normal size. They had also turned a greenish color... both of them. Cec said that the electricity had probably caused the bones to get infected. Sounded like a good diagnoses. Wasn't like I could come up with any better explanation. It was very unusual.

I tried to go on like nothing was wrong, but soon figured out if both your thumbs are almost as big as your hand it was hard to do anything. I tried to get Kenny help me zip my pants. He wasn't having any of it. My mother helped me.

When I got to the car, opening the door was another challenge. Driving was another. Opening the car door when I got to school was trying. My handwriting was even worse than normal, with me holding my pen like a three year old. Walking up and down the hallways looking for someone to accompany me to the restroom was kind of awkward. Finally Tommy Houy came to the rescue. He became my potty mate for the next few days. What are friends for? It never occurred to any of us that I may need to go to the doctor.

The Disease

It was in the hot summer time and I was out of school for the summer. I was about 14 or 15 years old and working for my Dad, Cecil Lewis. We were building a road down by Turkey Bend. Just country roads were all we built back then, hauling and spreading out caliche for new subdivision roads. I always ran the loader filling the five or six dump trucks that hauled the caliche. The trucks were driven mostly by our school age friends who were at least sixteen years old and could get a commercial license.

Socks Jackson was the mechanic and the foreman. It was his job to keep everyone and everything moving. He and Cec had grown up together. He was always around. A big part of my life and his favorite pass time was picking on me.

Since there wasn't a store for 20 miles around we always brought our lunch and had it under a big tree next to the caliche pit. As we were all together eating one day, Socks asked me, "What is that sore on your arm boy?" I didn't know, but my right arm just above the elbow had a small red irritated place on it.

The next day the sore had grown. Socks once again inquired and surmised that it was some disease, probably incurable, and would only get worse with time. Day after day the place continued to grow with Socks keeping a close watch on it for me. Within a couple of weeks, my whole upper arm was covered with this horrible sore and I was lying awake at night worrying. I couldn't think of anything else. I was sure Socks was right. The next thing all of my other extremities would start getting it too and then start falling off one by one. Even my privates could be affected, he would say.

Big Hanna, a neighbor lady, was Jimmy Palmer's momma, a nurse and my friend. She was always there to take up for me, since I was real small and Kenny, Jimmy, Socks and just about the rest of the world picked on me. I finally got nerve enough to get a second opinion from her. Immediately she told me that I had a burn on my arm. I said, "No way can that be right... it keeps getting a little worse each day and besides Socks told me what was going to happen ..." She assured me that it wasn't nearly as bad as Socks made it sound.

The next morning when I got on the loader I noticed an oily film on the right arm rest. A hydraulic relief valve was leaking and spraying a fine mist of oil and was coating my arm. The hot Texas sun was slowly baking my arm to well done. I probably would have noticed the oil on the armrest days earlier if

Socks had not occupied my mind so heavily with his prognosis. I simply laid a rag over the valve and it collected the oil. Within a few days my arm was well and my mind was more at ease.

Socks was always the kindest and most consider-ate person you ever met. He loved me dearly I know. I just don't think he realized the torment he put me through with his joking. Oh well, it taught me that there is a reason for everything.

~~~~~~~~~~

My Parents Cecil and Bonnie Gay

A Little Insight into Cecil Lewis

When I write about my Dad I hope I won't give the impression that Cecil Lewis was an outlaw or something. He was... what can I say... he was Cecil Lewis. A truly one-of-a-kind. If he liked you he'd do anything for you, if he didn't like you, he'd still do anything for you.

He was liked by most people, respected by many, but everyone knew to give him a wide berth. I owe much of my success to him. Not only in the things he taught me to do, but in the things I learned not to do. He was the nicest, yet meanest guy you ever met. He was tough yet had a tender heart. He was a good story teller but not always a very good listener. He loved his sons, but was always hard on us.

Just months before I graduated from High School my mother's sister was killed in a horrible car accident. Cec and my mother took our cousins Joy (4 years old) and Jan (9 months old) to raise. In the bringing up of his girls he morphed into a different person. It was sweet and amazing to watch.

The stories of Cecil Lewis are never ending. Bonnie Gay (he almost always addressed her that way) was the only person that could really cause him to stand at attention. She was a small lady, but had grit and determination. She was the glue that held us all together regardless of what happened. It's been almost a quarter of a century since she left us and I miss her daily. Cec lasted about 5 years longer, but never really adapted to life without her.

I can honestly say that while I missed him, in his later years his drinking had put a strain on our relationship; which seemed to make it easier to cope with his passing. Now with recalling all the stories about him, I am finally beginning to really miss him.

So please understand that I don't tell these

stories to disparage him in any way. They are being told because he can't. If he were here, he would be telling them himself, with laughter mixed in, like only Cecil Lewis could do.

~~~~~~~~~~

My Dad & Melvin Had Been Life Long Friends

Melvin Heine & my Dad, Cecil Lewis was just about as close as friends get. They were at one or the other's house for coffee almost every morning. Whatever Melvin owned, my Dad was welcome to use; that went both ways and included Cecil's two sons. Melvin and his wife never had children. When Melvin needed help hauling hay, building fence, or whatever, Cecil was more than happy to volunteer my bother & me. That's the way friends were.

It didn't set right with me the hot summer day that Melvin thought we weren't working hard enough hauling hay. His way of motivating us was to say, "If you boys don't hurry up, I'll just get Cecil to leave y'all here with me when he and your mother go to Yellowstone Park on vacation next week."

I am not sure whether we worked any faster or not, but that remark didn't set very well with me. I was no more than 14 years old then; now I can look back and see that Melvin was just trying to motivate two kids in the hay field, although I couldn't see it at the time. Melvin was the nicest, sweetest person, but it didn't seem that way back then.

A couple of days later we had our cattle in the pen. As we finished working the cows, my Dad told me to go to Melvin's and borrow his portable cattle sprayer so we could spray the cows before we turned them out.

Melvin lived a couple of miles down the road. When I pulled up, he was out by a little log crib where he kept his sprayer. When I told him what I was there for, in the most polite and nicest way possible he said, just back up here and I'll help you load it. As we swung it up on the tailgate Melvin said, "See these little screws here that hold the carburetor on, be sure to tighten them after you run it for a while. They will loosen up from the vibration."
"Okay, I'll do just that!" I replied.

As I drove back to our place a certain thought came over me. I could hardly wait to get there. As I pulled up and stepped out Cec was right there. I immediately launched in to this: "He said to tell you that you are welcome to borrow this equipment, but be sure we don't tear it up like we did everything else we ever borrowed."

"He said what? " So I repeated it and Cec exploded, "You take that G__D___ sprayer back and tell him to stick it straight up his A__!!! " (That's how Cecil Lewis talked when he was mad.) I was more than happy to deliver that message.

Melvin was sure surprised when I drove up not much more than ten minutes after I had left. He said, "Are y'all already finished spraying those cows?" Best I can remember, I repeated Cecil's words exactly. I unloaded the equipment and was on my way back home before Melvin could even utter a word.

Cecil and Melvin never again visited each morning for coffee as before and we never did haul hay or build fence for him again. As I look back, I don't remember ever meeting a kinder and more considerate person than Melvin Heine. In later years they did visit on occasion. I don't know that they ever discussed what had transpired over the sprayer.

Now I think how sad it is when grownups fail to talk about such matters. As a man with five sons this story reminded me to always check out their stories before I make any grand judgments. Sometimes a few words can alter the friendship of many years.

~~~~~~~~~~

Cecil Lewis & the Soldier

Although Cecil was our Dad, my brother and I called him Cec. No one else did. It was our name for him. He was from the old school as they say. He had a very rough exterior. Come to think of it he had a rough interior too. He was in the construction and trucking businesses. He worked hard his whole life. I always thought he was the toughest man I knew. He never backed away from anything, or anybody.

Once when I was about 13 or 14 my friend Billy Gene Henry and I accompanied Cec on a trip to collect a debt for some dozer work he had performed. He had arranged to meet the man that sold the piece of property where the work was done and the new owner who had just bought it. Also present was the real estate agent that had closed the deal. That was good because he is the one who had contacted Cec about doing the work.

The meeting took place at the Copperhead Inn in Jonestown, Tx. This was not exactly the place you would take the family for a nice afternoon, if you know what I mean. A bottle of Jack Daniel's was sitting in the center of table when we walked in. As the meeting got underway, each man would pour some whiskey in a shot glass and pass it to the next.

The real estate man and the other two began to argue about who was really responsible for paying for the work. It really seemed that no one wanted to own up to owing the money. Cec was content with listening to the back and forth, as long as the whiskey held out.

While this was taking place on the inside, Billy Gene and I were lingering around on the outside in the front of the place. From where the men sat they could see us through a large plate glass window. Our lingering turned into leaning against a car parked directly in front of the window. Suddenly a guy in his early twenties burst out of the door of the tavern yelling, "Keep your little asses off of my new car!" As he approached us he continued on with, "In fact don't even be looking at my car!"

Fort Hood was an hour's drive away, so the soldiers from there frequented Jonestown and the Lake Travis area on their time off. From his haircut and the way he dressed he was one of them. There were four or five other soldiers sitting at a table across the room from my Dad and his group.

Shortly afterwards we walked back inside and Cec asked us what had happened outside. We told him exactly what the soldier had said. Ever so calmly he arose from the table, walked to the door, and made his way to the front of the soldier's car. The sidewalk was high along the front of the parking area coming up well above the bumper of the cars parked next to it. Cec lifted his foot and stepped on the hood of the soldier's car and walked across the top; when he reached the trunk he did an about face and returned to the front then stepped back to the sidewalk.

Just as calmly as he had walked out, he walked back in. All of this in full view of both tables. He slowly strolled over to the soldier's table and said, "Don't you ever again say a damn word to my son you weaselly little bastard." Completely stunned at what had just happened, the whole table sat in silence.

He returned to his meeting and took a seat. Nothing was said for a few minutes. The soldiers got up and left. The real estate agent whipped out his checkbook and wrote the check. Handing it to him he said, "Cecil, I know you did the work and you should be paid. I'll collect from one of these bastards myself." With that done we got in the pickup and headed back to Smithwick.

~~~~~~~~~~

In-Grown Toenails

As a teenager I was plagued with ingrown toenails. They came and went. One day when I was complaining about the pain, probably using it as an excuse to get out of work, my dad had heard enough. "Come here boy, I am gonna fix those toes of yours!"

As I sat in the kitchen floor, he brought out a syringe that we had recently used while castrating hogs. It had the largest and coarsest needle you can even imagine. He loaded that syringe full of the same medicine we had used for deadening the hogs, then stuck that needle in the end of my big toe. It felt like fire. Since both toes were afflicted I knew what was coming next. When Cecil Lewis decided to do something there was no changing his mind. I didn't even try.

I don't believe hog medicine is made to be used on humans. It sure didn't seem to deaden the pain, or at least he hadn't given it enough time. In his mind it was time to operate. He used an extra-large pair of toenail clippers. They looked more like something you'd trim trees with than dig out an ingrown toenail. He dug in. At that moment I knew how the fellows on Gunsmoke felt when Doc Adams cut bullets out of them while they were fully awake.

Cec worked feverishly while sitting on his patient's chest to hold me down. With surgery finally over, he bathed my feet in alcohol. I'm here to tell you this wasn't like Jesus bathing the feet of his disciples. After the bleeding had mostly stopped, he poured merthiolate all over them, used a roll of gauze on each toe, and taped them up. He was ready for the healing to begin.

Best I can remember it was about two weeks before I could wear a shoe on either foot. The method he used didn't really work, as my condition returned within a few months. But I never did complain around him again.

It took several years before I got my courage up to do anything about my toes. When I was about 30 years old, I went to real a podiatrist and had him do it. There was pain associated with it that time, but at least the needle wasn't the worst part. So for the last half of my life I've been ingrown toe nail free.

~~~~~~~~~~

Cec and the Riviera

Kenny, Cec, and I headed off one Saturday morning to buy Kenny a new car to go to college in. Cec was sure that Kenny should have something economical, so a nice 63 Oldsmobile Cutlass 4 door was acquired for him. It was a pretty common looking little car, more like one our grandmother should have been driving. Kenny was less than pleased, but knew that life was going to be tough for him, with his going to school and plans to get married soon. So he went along.

On the same lot was a 1965 Buick Rivera. This was in 1968, so the Rivera was only three years old. I was sure it would cost too much, but I made the suggestion to Cec that I really needed that car since I was going into my junior year of high school. For some strange reason, upon finding it priced at just under $2,000, he agreed that I could buy it. I am still not sure why, as that was a lot of money for a kid in the sixties. He surely felt that I would pay for it somehow.

That car had everything in the way of gadgets that had ever been thought of for a car. It turned out to be a fine purchase, at least for a few months. I drove that car hard. After about six months, the situation with the Rivera started to unravel when the engine blew up. All Cec said was, "Boy you jest gonna have to put a new engine in it."

I brought it into our shop and started tearing it down. With a 465 Cu. In. engine and all the gadgets it had on it, it was a task that I wasn't sure I could handle. You can't even imagine the hoses and wires under that hood. But unaided by anyone, I finally got the new motor in it and it actually ran.

Now on to the next problem... the engine vibrated so badly you couldn't hold it on the road. The engine I had installed turned out to be defective, but it did have a guarantee. All I had to do was pull it all back out and the company would exchange it. I was better at doing it the second time around. This time, it ran fine.

I no sooner got the motor running again, than the transmission started slipping. It wasn't slipping too badly, but Cec told me to get ready, I would have to replace it soon. His fatherly advice was to just wreck it and we would collect the insurance.

Cec had a different way of thinking than a lot of other people. He really didn't see anything wrong with making an insurance company pay, because nearly everything he made ended up going to the IRS, a Bank, or Insurance Companies. "Boy, you just need to wreck that damn thing before it gets to where it won't move."

At the time I worked after school for the Chevrolet & Buick dealership. I was the handyman around the car lot. I kept the batteries charged, the dust off the cars, moved cars from place to place, and ran back odometers when a car came in that showed a few too many miles.

Each night as I started my nine mile drive home, I would be determined to straighten out the next curve. However, by the time I got there, I would decide that Hamilton Creek would serve my needs if I just cut past the end of the guardrail and run into the backup waters of the lake. As I approached Hamilton Creek, it occurred to me that Sycamore Creek, with its big boulders laying all up and down the creek bed would serve my needs much better. And you guessed it, by the time I got to Sycamore I had a better plan for down the road. Well the next thing I knew, I was already sitting in front of the house.

This happened several days in a row. By the time I got home I would be a teenage walking-talking-frazzle. I guess the pressure was too much for me. Doing dangerous things usually didn't bother me, but this seemed a little over the top. Each time Cec saw that I still hadn't done the deed, he'd just smile and shake his head as I assured him I would do it the next day.

Well I put it off until one morning when I got

ready to leave for school, the ole Rivera wouldn't move out of its tracks. I caught a ride to school then walked across the street to work at the car lot. About the time I was getting off work Kenny drove into the car lot and his first words were, "Don't worry about your Riviera anymore, Cec just totaled it out."

He went on to explain that Cec had told him to push the Riviera with him in it into town, a distance of nine miles, with the bumper of a pickup. We had done this a number of times because we found ourselves broken down a lot back in those days. Cec was always the impatient kind, so as Kenny pushed he was constantly motioning for him to push faster and faster. At the top of Whitman Hill, he waved Kenny off. Kenny thought he was just going to coast on down the hill and let Kenny catch him in the next flat to start the pushing again. Kenny was dead wrong about Cec's intentions.

As he was about mid-way down the hill coming to a curve Cec pulled to the edge of the road, opened the door going about 25 or 30 miles per hour, and rolled out. Kenny tells that he tumbled and rolled for quite a distance. Startled as to what had just occurred, Kenny pulled up to check on our poor old Dad. He was scraped and torn, his wire rim glasses wadded up on his head. All Cec said was, "Get the hell out of here before someone comes along."

Meanwhile Cec decided to go down and inspect the condition of the car. Sure enough the car came to rest on a huge boulder after going off of a fifty-foot drop-off. As he pulled himself back to the top, someone came along and gave him a ride back home. From there he called the sheriff's office and told them a crazy driver had run him off the road. He met a deputy back at the scene and you would think the story would end there; but not with Cecil Lewis.

The car was towed to George Becker's wrecking yard, where it sat for several months. Cec would drive past it several times each day. He finally rea-soned that one day someone would come along and want to buy the transmission out of that car. If they did, it would be discovered that it was completely burned up. So he went to George Becker and bought the whole car for $500, the salvage price.

Then he hauled it home and put it down in our pasture for several years. I am not sure what hap-pened to that car. I am sure that George Becker would have rebuilt the transmission for $500, the price Cec paid to buy it back. But you know, that sure wouldn't have been Cecil Lewis, and the story wouldn't have been nearly so memorable.

The Stolen Beer Caper

Big Jimmy grew up across the highway from our Grandmother in Smithwick and helped Kenny & me haul hay and do other work around the place as we grew up. After getting his commercial driver's license he started driving a dump truck for our Dad on weekends and after school. Since Kenny always had a girlfriend and was usually occupied with her, Jimmy and I hung out together a lot. He was three years older than me, but we got along pretty well, especially when Kenny wasn't around. Big Jimmy was always real big for his age, so I felt like he was someone good to hang out with. He was about as oversized as I was under-sized for our ages.

A couple of boys my age (who shall remain name-less) broke into a store and stole all the beer and cigarettes they could haul off. They hid the beer down under some rock ledges below a road on the way to one of the boys' house. Big Jimmy was told about the beer and its location by the two. They were hoping to make a dollar or two a case off of it and thought with Jimmy being older and out of school already, he would be the perfect person to help them dispose of it.

That was probably a good plan on their part... until he told me about it. I immediately asked Jimmy to go with me to see if the beer was really there. I had a 1966 El Camino at the time and it was Travis Peak here we come! That was the little community where the beer was hidden. Upon arriving at the location, flashlight in hand, I went to take a look. Sure enough case upon case of beer was stashed under the rock ledges just as they had told Jimmy. I threw a couple of cases up and hollered for him to put the beer in the back of the El Camino. As soon as he got it loaded there was more there for him to load. In a few minutes I had handed up the last case that I could locate. When I got back up to road level, I dis-covered the rear of the El Camino was level-full of beer. Some of just about every brand I had ever heard of.

About that time the two beer thieves drove up. They couldn't believe how well everything was coming together, seeing all the beer leaving so quickly. When they ask Jimmy how much they would be getting, he just shrugged and turned to me. I let them know we wouldn't be paying them or anyone else for stolen beer, and since it was already in my pickup, I consid-ered it mine. I was sure they weren't going to run home and tell their parents or go to the cops com-plaining.

Off we headed for Smithwick discussing where all this beer could safely be hidden. We finally drove down into Ms. Ollie Cox's place, thinking we could leave it there. We found a big mesquite tree that looked like a good place to hide it. After unloading a few cases and drinking a few of the beers, we decided that with deer hunters coming soon to start building stands they would end up with all the beer instead of us. We loaded everything back up, and took off to a safer spot. Then it hit me like a ton of bricks. Our basement at home would offer the perfect hiding place.

It was nearing midnight by that time and my parents were sound asleep. I backed right up to the front door. With all the commotion Cec was soon standing there with a dazed look on his face. "What in the hell are you boys doing?" After explaining to him what had taken place, he carried more beer to the basement than either one of us. He was like a kid in a candy store. My mother, Bonnie Gay, just stood there shaking her head in disbelief. We never actually counted them, but I think there may have been at least 60 to 70 cases of beer. Plenty to keep us all happy for a while.

The two culprits never did have a very high opinion of me after that. I told them they were lucky that I didn't smoke or I would have made them turn over the cigarettes too. I guess we were kind of like the Smithwick mafia.

A Typical Friday Night Growing Up in Marble Falls in the 60's

We would drive through town, go up the roadside park on the hill south of town, turn around then drive to the far north end of town. Turn around and repeat that same course dozens of times during a Friday or Saturday night. The whole circle was no more than a couple of miles. Very few cars would speed, mostly just cruising up and down looking cool. Gasoline cost 35 cents per gallon, so for $5.00 you could drive around all night long.

Most of us were drinking beer and having a good ole time. There were drugs in those days, mostly marijuana which was easy to stay away from. If you found like-minded friends who weren't interested in smoking pot you didn't feel pressured to do so. But beer drinking was everywhere and the consumption of various hard liquors was common as well.

If you wanted to speed, that took place on any of the four main highways leading from town. We would take off out of town, open it up to see what top speed could be obtained... speeds of 120, 130 and 140 mph being common. We even had a stretch of road-way to the south and another to the west where we had marked off what was roughly a $\frac{1}{4}$ mile. That was where we would have drag races.

Almost any night a few cars would go out to one of the strips and have a face-off. Most of the time we were cautious not to linger too long after a race just in case the squealing of tires had been heard by a City Marshall, or a County Deputy. We didn't have a fulltime DPS officer until late in the 60's. Very seldom did you see more than one officer patrolling the streets of Marble Falls. A lot of the time you may not see one all night long.

I suppose the 60's were a time when many of the Dads were in some way trying to re-live their youth through the sons. It almost seems that many of us drove cars that were much beyond our parent's abilities to pay for. Back then the monthly payments for a nice car was $125 to $150, which in today's dollars doesn't seem like much, but a good wage for a working man was $200 per week. Yet, the streets were full of shiny new Malibu's, Mustangs, Road-runner's, GTO's, Charger's and everything else that is termed a muscle car today.

On this one particular Friday night when I was in my junior year of high school, my best friend Tommy and I made a night of it in his 68 Roadrunner. During that span of time we had decided to do something much more exotic than just drink beer. We would fill an ice chest with finely crushed ice and add a couple of gallons of Bali Hai wine. When the wine was poured over the crushed ice it was very much like driving around eating snow cones all night; very fruity tasting. If you consumed enough of the snow cones you could begin to do things that you would regret.

One might ask how I remember that this story took place on a Friday night? My brother, being a college freshman, was due to come home for the weekend and was bringing his new roommate. I had heard stories of this roommate's car, a 68 Dodge Charger with a 440 CI engine that he had equipped with dual 4 barrel carburetors. You didn't have to know much to know big motor plus 2 four's was going to run very fast. We drove around knowing sometime after 9:00 or 10:00 pm that brother and roommate, Otis, would come rolling in.

Marble Falls, being a resort type town only an hour's drive from Ft. Hood (the largest military base in the country) had soldiers around often. A Plymouth Roadrunner with two soldiers in it pulled up alongside us to inquire if we would like to have a little match off on the drag strip for a $25. My friend Tommy wasn't into racing that night, or any other night. He was very careful and gentle with his 383 Roadrunner. So we declined the offer and moved on. The soldiers continue to rip up and down through town challenging everyone without finding a taker.

Finally we pulled in to one of the local hangouts, The Yacht Restaurant. Sitting next to us were the two army guys. A conversation ensued, a few insults were thrown around, but nothing that wasn't expected. When the subject finally came around that, "No one in this little shit hole of a town would take them on...." I told them to hold on for an hour or so and someone would be arriving that I was willing to bet $100 on. Big talk from me I guess, but I knew the roommate had a reputation of showing off his car anytime he got the chance and the car the soldiers were in was a fairly stock Plymouth. Seemed like a safe bet to me. They took the bet.

The college boys finally arrived. When Otis revved the engine on that hot Charger the ground shook. Didn't take soldier boy long to start trying to weasel out on the bet. I wasn't going for it. A bet is a bet. Words flew. Threats were made. With the soldier sitting in his car and me standing by the door I decided that dragging him out of his window and taing the $100 from him may be the only choice I had.

The Bali Hai wine has something in it that makes you a little bigger and a little meaner than you probably are. At the same time I suppose military training teaches you not to let your enemy take you captive, instead pull a gun out as if you are serious about a fire fight. And that is what he did. It was a large black semi-automatic looking thing. It should have been more intimidating than it was.

Instead of backing away, returning to our car, and heading down the road for another snow cone I decided to taunt soldier boy holding the gun. I had noticed that every time I let words fly and he would start to raise his gun, his buddy would grab his hand and hold it down on the console. Hold it down without much effort, is what it looked like. This seemed like a weakness on my opponent's part. That only embold- ened me more so I began screaming for this big bad soldier boy to shoot me. "Come on big brave soldier just use that gun if you think you can!" It was the Bali Hai at work. Next thing I know he fired up the Roadrunner and hauls it out of the parking lot. I was thinking, "So this who is protecting our country?"

The next morning when I woke up I lay there reflecting on the previous night. I was nauseous and my head was still spinning from the Bali Hai. I knew something very crazy and amazing had happened. Even being a sixteen year old kid, I knew I had pushed fate to its limit. If my memory serves me correctly, that was the last time I ever over indulged in Bali Hai snow cones.

~~~~~~~~~~

The Rattlesnake Bite Victim

Cec allowed an old fellow from Marble Falls to establish a wrecking yard on a little patch of ground on our property. Old Man Hugh Hampton was as nice a fellow as I ever met, and a very hard worker. He was honest as the day was long. (Whatever that saying is supposed to mean.)

Hugh had a fellow working for him up in the junk yard pulling usable parts off cars. It was in the summertime, because Kenny and I were both at the house. I'm betting we had stopped by to grab a bite to eat. We weren't there making a leisurely day of it I'm sure. All of a sudden the worker and a boy (11 or 12 years old) pulled up to the house in a panic. The man had been bitten by a rattlesnake. Could we get him to the hospital? Of course we could. We all four piled in the front seat of a 58 Ford Pickup, the vehicle Kenny was currently driving. Away we went, headed to the Emergency Room in Burnet some 25 miles away.

Kenny was driving more normal for him than the junkyard worker would have thought. He had the old Ford wound up. The worker wasn't enjoying the trip at all, between the bite and being scared half to death. The Hamilton Creek Bridge, a couple of miles east of Marble Falls, was narrow. Two cars could meet on the bridge but it was intimidating. On each side of the bridge was a 3' tall concrete wall along the edge, forming a barrier to keep cars from running off of the side.

Sightseeing was popular on that road and had caused an oncoming car to stop right at the end of the bridge. Another vehicle approached the stopped car from behind and not realizing how fast we were traveling decided to pass in our lane. Through something between great driving skills, and dumb luck Kenny avoided colliding with the vehicle in our lane. It did cause our old Ford pickup to fly up onto the concrete barrier and travel the length of the bridge with our front bumper gliding on top of the wall. All of this happened in the span of less than five seconds. That left the rattlesnake bite victim in the floor of the pickup, even more scared than ever. I just remember him saying "Please slow down, I'd rather die of a snake bite than be killed in a car wreck!"

I'm not sure Kenny slowed down that much. For some reason we decide to go by Dr. Sheppard's office in Marble Falls to seek help. Upon arriving there they told us to go on to Burnet. I'm sure that was to the further horror of the snake bite victim. But we got the guy and boy delivered to the hospital and then went on about our day.

The Runaway Tractor

We always had a problem with trucks, cars and machinery taking off and rolling away when we parked it at our house. We didn't live on top of a hill exactly, but the ground wasn't level either. Which was good and bad. Bad if the brakes weren't set good, but good when the battery was down on a vehicle and you needed to roll it to get it started. Most of the time everything worked out without a real disaster.

Once I started to town, forgot something and came back. Forgetting to set the parking brake and in a hurry to get to a party I ran inside; a few seconds later I heard the crash. The little Pontiac car hit the house right at the kitchen. Our house was pretty sturdy so the wall withstood the impact, but the kitchen cabinets were knocked out from the wall about a half a foot. I asked Cec if he needed me to stay and help put them back in place. He told me to good ahead and be sure to enjoy myself at the party. (Or either get your #%^*** on out of here and I'll get it fixed) The next morning it was all fixed and the subject never came back up.

When my little teenage girl cousin, who had come to live with us, was learning to drive Cec put her in a Plymouth that had a push button transmission. One day she parked and a little later came back out to leave... no car. I came along about that time and she thought I was messing with her and had hidden it.

Knowing I hadn't I found out where it had been parked then tracked it through some broken bran-ches of scrub brush going off toward a stock tank. Standing on the bank I saw a light glow out in the middle. The car was brown, but had a white top. The water was about 10-12 feet deep. Through the murk-iness the glow I could see the top of the car. In a matter of a few minutes I had dived down, attached a winch cable to it and we were pulling it out.

We drained the oil and fuel tank, dried it all out for a couple of days then filled it back up. It fired up and Cec kept that car around for several years.

You just didn't want to leave the windows up on a hot day. It sure wouldn't smell very good inside.

Several other trucks and machines ran away, but only a few of them were really costly to fix afterwards. The one that stands out in my mind the most is an Allis Chalmers model "C" Tractor. Kenny had been doing some work with the tractor when a couple of fellows came along that were going to go hunting down in our lower pasture and needed to be shown where to hunt. Kenny parked the tractor out from the house on a grade so he could roll it to start instead of cranking it when he got ready to go back to work.

After getting the hunters situated, we drove back up to the tractor only the tractor wasn't there. About then we looked down the way to where our Aunt Netta had a mobile home parked. It had been there long enough to be landscaped around and nice flagstone sidewalk built up to the front door. That was about 150 yards from where the tractor was parked. When it rolled down hill, it traveled up the sidewalk and jumped up a set of steps.

The tractor was configured with a set of narrow wheels on the front. When it finally came to a stop those front wheels and engine compartment had passed through the door with no more than 2" to spare.

The tires stopped only a couple of inches from a sofa that was positioned directly in front of the door. The back tires were only two inches from entering the front door. It was evident that if any part of the tractor had been an inch or two wider or greater in length, more than likely the mobile home would have been a total loss. All that it needed was a $10 piece of wooden trim to repair the door stop where the screen door was pushed inward, instead opening to the outside. Anyone who saw it, or the pictures, agreed that it was the most amazing thing they had ever seen.

~~~~~~~~~~

Dean and Fred's 57 Chevy

It was just before mid-night on New Year's Eve. We weren't just ushering in a new year, but a new decade. Dean, Tommy and I were at The Circle Inn. Not usually a place where teens hung out; Alice didn't allow it. There was a regular clientele that went there, but this night was different. It was a very festive occasion. The place was packed. I was shooting pool with someone whose name doesn't come to mind.

We had ridden out there with Dean and he wanted to go down the road to the 281 Club where his folks where ringing in the New Year. I'm not sure why he thought it was a good idea to come over and disrupt the pool game by taking his arm and raking the balls in the pockets. It was his way of prying me away from the game but instead it caused me to go upside of my very dear friend's head with a pool cue. Alice, my future grandmother-in -law, soon had collared us both and had us out in the parking lot.

Just about then some old man, dressed in western attire with bolo tie and all, was standing in front of Dean and me. Neither of us knew him, but he was holding what appeared to be a nickel plated revolver, and having a hard time keeping his balance because he was very drunk. Pointing the gun at us, he said, "Leave that boy alone, do you hear me, leave that boy alone!" We were confused because we were both just boys and didn't have a clue which one of us he found it neces-sary to protect. Using the best judgment we could find at the moment we just rushed him and wrestled the pistol out of his hand. We handed the gun to Alice and got in the car to leave.

The car was an immaculately restored 57 2-door Chevrolet. It belonged to Dean's cousin Fred. He had left it at the Schaefer home while he was away in the service, I think the Air Force. Why the keys were left to where Dean, home on leave, could find them I'll never understand.

Dean driving, Tommy up front, me in the back. Dean said something that I didn't agree with so I reached up, grabbed him around the neck, and pulled him over the seat. The only problem was the toes of Dean's shoes caught the headliner and when he arrived in the back seat so did the headliner. When we discovered the mess we had the fight left us both.

There was no way for Dean to take the car back and pretend it never happened. Fred was pretty hot about the incident. We each had to come up with $125 to replace the headliner. I saw Fred not that long ago and mentioned the headliner incident. He still seemed a little miffed at Dean.

~~~~~~~~~~

Dean Came Home From Boot Camp

Dean and I ran around together. My brother and his sister dated through high school so that connection threw us together. They eventually married after high school. Dean was a little older than me so he had left school to join the Army when he became eligible, but I was still just sixteen years old and a sophomore in high school.

After completing basic training Dean came in on leave. He and several of our friends came out and picked me up to celebrate his return. It was a Saturday afternoon around 2:00 PM. They were in Larry Joe's little Mercury Meteor. Besides Dean and Larry, there was Jimmy, JW and another one or two. We were packed in that little car.

Jimmy was older than the rest of us, but still a ways from being legal age to buy liquor. But he looked older so we headed straight for Johnson City, the closest place to purchase liquor back then. All the others had him get them vodka, or rum, or something that would make good tasting drinks. I said, "Get me a fifth of Old Crow..." and Dean said the same for him. Wanting to press Dean a little I added, "...and also a pint!" and Dean said he wanted a pint also. Maybe we brought out the worst in each other.

As we drove across the bridge at the Pedernales River, leaving northbound out of Johnson City, I threw the empty pint bottle out. Shortly thereafter Dean did the same. As we got back to Round Mountain, a 15-mile trip, I was finishing off the fifth. I guess you could say I was a showoff. I am not sure why I was in such a hurry, but I guess I didn't want some Army boy thinking he could out drink me.

We turned down a little country road, just for some good out of the way partying. It must have been 4:00 PM by that time. I remember a few miles down the road that we made a pit stop. The whiskey must have hit bottom about then, because after that I don't remember anything until just before daylight the next morning.

When I woke up I had a strange feeling that I was in a place very foreign to me. As I swung out of my bed, my feet hit a cold metal floor. My underwear was wadded up around my ankles. That was all I had on. It didn't take long for me to realize I was in jail. But where? The door to my cell was left unlocked so I made my way to a window in a larger enclosure. The streetlights below lit the Town Square. But nothing looked familiar. I had never been at that vantage point. Later I found out that I was actually in the Burnet County Jail. Yes, Sheriff Wallace Riddell's jail. The main confusion for me was why do they take young boys pants off when they put them in jail?

A little later that morning, when the Sheriff came in to discuss my current situation with me, I posed that question to him. That is when he delivered the news to me that I was in that condition when I arrived there. I don't think that made me feel any better. He asked who he should call. I ask him to call my Dad and please tell him I needed clothes. He told me that Dean was also in there, but had arrived with his clothes on. Knowing Dean was there too brought some measure of happiness to me. I guess I didn't want to be the only one. Him arriving clothed and me naked didn't make me feel much better. But at the moment I had more troubling things to worry about... I was really sick.

I was served a bowl of oatmeal for breakfast, but couldn't eat so I set it aside. For some reason, I was coughing up little gravels and sand. The same substance was packed in my nostrils and ears. I also had welts and stings over every inch of my body. Later I found out the reason.

Soon after I lost consciousness the car load of us ended up down by the river above Marble Falls. My friends, trying to take care of me in my drunken state, took me out of the hot car and left me on the ground, not noticing that I was lying in a red ant den. After a while, when someone noticed I was covered with ants, they removed my clothes and threw me in the river, hoping to rid me of the ants. I guess they thought that may help sober me up a little; instead I sank to the bottom.

Luckily, the water was shallow with a sandy gravel bar coming up to the edge, so they were able to see me lying there on the bottom and pulled me out. Perhaps not thinking to get my clothes they just loaded me back into the car. Dean had passed out long before. Not wanting to drive around all night with us in

the back seat, they drove to the roadside park over-
looking Marble Falls, parked the car, and left us in it.
They then got a ride with someone else and took off.

Noticing that the Mercury had been left sitting
the City Marshall decided to check it out. When he
found us we were loaded into the back of the police
car and driven around town until someone identified
us. Then they hauled us off to Burnet. The Sheriff
lived on the bottom floor of the jail, so when a pris-
oner was brought in they entered through the living
quarters. They were having a family get together
when we were brought in; two drunk teenagers, one
naked. The Sheriff was not happy with the situation.

After he got the call my dad and brother brought
clothes for me to wear. Dean's dad picked him up and
we all had to go to the Marble Falls City Hall. We
were charged with several offenses each and me one
extra one. A deal was struck for the charges to be
dropped if we didn't get into trouble again. I never
had any problems related to that incident. Either
there wasn't really a record kept, or it was overlooked in the future.

I did get teased a lot when I got to school that
Monday and for a long time afterwards. But it wasn't
all bad. In today's terms I received a lot of street
creds. Since then I have never been able to stand

the smell of whiskey. That was probably a good thing. The ant bites went away within a few days. The irregular heartbeat I had for a while finally became normal.

The strangest thing was, when they arrived in Burnet to pick me up, my dad wasn't really upset, but Kenny had smoke pouring out of his ears. He thought I must have been the stupidest kid alive and was mad about the embarrassment he was going to endure.

Some years later while talking to Wallace Riddell about that incident, he helped me understand why my dad was as understanding as he was. When Cec was a teenager Wallace had found him swimming naked in a stock tank at the edge of Burnet. He was totally inebriated and Wallace hauled him over to his place for a night upstairs.

My real punishment was when I got home and had to look my mother in the face. She didn't say a word. She didn't have to. I could see the concern in her eyes. Before I was grown I saw it many more times. I think she just silently prayed that all would work out and it did.

~~~~~~~~~~

The 58 Ford Pickup

It's funny the ideas that young boys can have. Living about 9 miles out of Marble Falls meant a drive home every night on a very crooked stretch of paved country road. It's common knowledge that deer feed at night by the moon. So on a moonlit night there are more deer along the roadway. We were convinced that on a night when the moon was really bright that driving home without headlights provided an overall chance of not hitting a deer. With headlights off you could see the silhouette of deer alongside and in the road. We figured that deer became excited at seeing headlights and reacted by running, many times directly into the path of your car.

Late at night was our usual time for heading home. It wasn't unusual to make the nine mile trip without seeing another car. Without your headlights on you could easily see the glow of any oncoming car lights from far away allowing you to turn your lights on well before meeting. Meeting a car with your headlights off was a definite no-no. This one night Kenny left out of town in the 58 Ford pickup at the same time that Big Jimmy, with me as a passenger, left heading to Smithwick in his 53 model Red Chevy pickup.

After clearing out of town, both sets of lights were turned off. It was a nice night. As crooked as the road was, there was one straight section that we called the mesquite flats. It was the area where you were almost guaranteed to see deer. Speeds were average that night, reaching 80 to 90 MPH. Only because that was about as fast as either of those vehicles would run. Kenny was in the lead a couple of hundred yards ahead of Jimmy and me.

You must understand that braking systems were much different in those days, before antilock brakes. It wasn't uncommon to press the brake pedal and need to give it a couple of pumps to get the best braking action. Many times, with the lack of self-adjusting brakes, pushing the pedal really hard would cause one wheel to lockup, causing erratic behavior of the vehicle.

Suddenly, as we were almost to the end of mesquite flats, Jimmy and I saw the flash of red tail lights in front of us. Then the left taillight became the right taillight. Sparks flew as metal contacted asphalt. The tail lights continued to swap sides as contents from the pickup bed scattered all along the highway and the side of the road. Jimmy reacted by turning his lights back on and the old Ford finally came to rest on its side. Battered and bruised Kenny climbed out, shaken but not seriously hurt. All this as a result of several deer in the middle of the road.

Within minutes a chain, one of the many scattered items, was hooked to the back bumper of the Chevy and to a location on the underside of the Ford. A nice tug and a couple of jerks later, the Ford was upright and on all fours. We raised the hood and up righted the battery that wasn't secured in. We could see that some oil had spilled out, but hoping that it wasn't too much Kenny fired it off. It ran fine, but smoked a little more than normal. After picking up all the contents we could find and throwing them in the back of the truck, we headed home knowing we'd be back on the scene as daylight broke to get any remaining rem-nants that couldn't be located in the dark.

The old pickup was scratched and dented, but still ran. It already had its battle scars from the previous encounter with the bridge railing during the wild ride with the snake bite victim. That encounter had left its front bumper almost completely ground off on the right side.

Amazingly that old truck was around for a while longer before ending up in Hugh Hampton's Wrecking Yard. They just don't build em like they used to.

~~~~~~~~~~

Bexar County Deputy

This incident happened in 1970 shortly before I graduated. I had a 68 model Red SS Camaro-396-4 speed. Kenny was in on leave from the Army. Our friend Butch was also coming in on leave and was arriving at the San Antonio Airport. He and Kenny were the same age but I counted him as a friend as well. I always hung out with Kenny. In fact I was like his American Express Card until him and that red headed chick hooked up. Yeah, 'He Never Left Home Without Me.'

Kenny and I were able to get a lot of catching up done on the trip down to pick up Butch and thought we all three would get a lot more done on the return trip. Butch landed and we gathered up all of his belongings. He was sprawled out in the cramped backseat, with me driving, and Kenny passengering.

We came out of SA north bound on 281. A short distance out of town, I remember meeting a cop car, but we were going well under the speed limit, so I knew we were all good. But in just a few seconds the cop car was flying up behind us with lights flashing. I was positive we had done nothing so when he got right on my bumper I continued driving, knowing there was a roadside park a very short distance ahead. We pulled off, he pulled in behind us. The first thing I heard was him racking a shell in the chamber of his shotgun. "Keep your hands where I can see them and all of you step out!" I knew we hadn't done anything. Maybe driving the extra few hundred yards had ticked him off, but him holding a shotgun on us?

He had us move around in front of my car. "Get your driver's license out and lay them on the hood..." was his instructions. He wasn't in command like you think he would be. He seemed nervous, to the point of shaking. He was trying to hold the shotgun with one hand and his revolver with the other. It was a Barney Fife moment.

We each took our license out, one at a time and place them on the hood. Kenny was the last to get his out. He flung it towards the hood rather than laying it there. It sailed and hit the ground. Deputy was irritated. I asked him to please calm down and don't shoot us; then for permission to pick up the license. He let me. We told him why we were where we were. Kenny and Butch could each show him their Military ID's. That started to turn the tide.

Three boys had escaped from a Juvenile Detention Facility at Gatesville and were believed to be headed to San Antonio to kill one of their parents With definite evidence we weren't them, he went back to his patrol car and we followed. He showed us the handwritten note he had made of the make, model, color and license plate number. While it wasn't an exact match it was eerily similar. It was easy to see why he had mistaken us for the other boys.

That has been about 45 years ago. For some strange reason I still remember his name. It was Deputy Bill White. After talking awhile and him realizing we were from Marble Falls he told us his folks lived at Kingsland. He had often stopped at the Texaco Station where I had worked.

~~~~~~~~~~~

A Note About My Brother

As you read these stories please understand that many of the participants are no longer with us, or lack the computer skills needed to get on Facebook. Even though Kenny Lewis falls into the latter group he will now surely read at least some of these stories. Kenny and my stories generally travel closely down some trivial, inconsequential detail. I'm sure reading *The Flying Stick* he'll correct me to say, "The stick hit you in the head before it whacked me in the ear..." or something like that. I think it's the older child syndrome, needing to always be right.

The Flying Stick

It was my 16th year of life. My brother Kenny was in his second semester of college up at Tarleton. He had moved into an apartment that had formerly been occupied by a cop who had left a night stick behind. Kenny was sure that I would need that club one day so he brought it home to me. He always looked out for me like that. The wooden stick had been drilled through the core and had a steel rod inserted. I kept it stuck between the seat and the console.

My means of transportation at that point was the 65 Buick Rivera. It was a Saturday and we had been down around Jonestown building a road. Kenny never cared much for my driving so when we headed back to Smithwick that afternoon he drove. He always drove fast; we all did in my family... even our mother.

Just as we came past Lago Vista where there is a long curve where the highway department had just started replacing all of the wooden bollard posts with reflectors that were common along roadways. They came up with what appeared to be flimsy little steel posts with the reflectors, like the ones that are still used today. Those spindly little posts just didn't seem all that sturdy to the two of us. Thinking we would test out their strength and durability I told Kenny to hand me the night stick.

I'm still not sure who we were trying to prove what to, but as we rounded the corner on the two lane road at 85 MPH, Kenny pulled close to the row of posts on my side. I leaned out and the stick made contact. The momentum that propelled that stick backwards was unbelievable. It hit my right arm, causing a one inch high bump to rise up along almost the entire length. The club then sailed back through the window and whacked Kenny on top of the right ear. It seemed like it bounced around forever, hitting me in the head and finally coming to rest in the backseat.

Dazed and addled, Kenny locked up the brakes and slid. Luckily there was a long level dirt area along the right side of the highway. We plowed up some ground before coming to a stop. Both doors flew open and we fell out kicking. Soon a line of cars were stopped wondering what had happened. I was hurting and Kenny had blood gushing from his ear was hurting too. After a bit we dusted off, climbed in, and headed for home.

Even with the steel core, the stick was still broken. So much for that.

~~~~~~~~~~

Boating

It was during the time Kenny was away serving in the Army. When he would come home we spent as much time together as we could. When he got home one time I had just purchased a Chrysler 17' fiberglass boat, light yellow, with a 55 HP Chrysler outboard motor. (Yes there was a time that Chrysler got in the boat business - not a real successful venture.)

It was used, but just gently so. Not a real powerful boat but it would cruise up and down the lake. Gasoline was well south of $.50 per gallon still. (For those unfamiliar with my terminology - that means it was costing less than 50 cents per gallon.)

We headed up to the lake from my south Austin home. Needing gas I stopped at a Texaco station at 290 and Westgate Blvd. This was the time before self-service. A little gal came bouncing out to fill us up. By the time we bought a couple of bottles of outboard oil, filled up two of the outboard gas tanks, and topped off my truck's tank the total bill came to just around $20.

Since I was furnishing the boat and pickup Kenny wanted to do his part and insisted on paying. Kenny and Karen were living on about $400 a month if I remember correctly; being in the Army wasn't going to make you rich. Reluctantly I agreed and Kenny handed her a fifty. As she turned to head inside to get his change, I said in my best Kenny Lewis voice, "Hey BABE, just keep the change!"

I immediately turned and got in the truck, as I heard her say, "Oh, my God, thank you so much!" Kenny was speechless. I worked in a gas station when I was a kid I think the most tip I ever got was a quarter. Tipping like that was unheard of.

~~~~~~

On the same day of the gas station tipping incident, Kenny and I launched the boat in upper Lake Travis at Smithwick. We had the boat and all the paraphernalia for an afternoon of tearing up the lake skiing... then it occurred to us that neither of us knew how to ski. We had grown up on that lake and spent as much time on the water as anyone; we just didn't do it standing up on a couple of boards.

We found a quiet area to start pulling each other. A 55 HP Chrysler Outboard isn't the perfect power source to learn how to ski behind. Learning to ski takes a certain amount of patience, especially from the boat driver. Kenny Lewis may be the only person to ever call Smithwick home that had less patience than Cecil Lewis, or Ronnie Lewis.

It got dark and we hadn't had much success. Not ones to give up easily, we continued on. For anyone that's ever been in a boat with Kenny Lewis driving you will understand why I learned to ski pretty quickly.

I learned how to ski out of self-preservation. You don't want Kenny swinging back around to pick you up in daylight hours, much less when it's dark. I just tried to stay up and ski to the bank where he could drive over and get me rather than take a chance of being run over in the middle of the lake.

Kenny never let me get ahead of him doing anything, so he followed suit staying up soon thereafter. Once we knew how to ski, we stayed with it and continued to ski until the wee hours of the morning. Lucky there was a nice moon.

~~~~~~~~~~

Delbert & Nancy Boultinghouse
(My Mother's Parents)

Much, if not all of their married life was spent in Smithwick. Nancy was a member of the Martin Family from Burnet. I think Delbert was raised primarily in Smithwick. The date of their marriage is unknown to me, but most likely it was around 1914 or 1915.

They lived on what has always been known as the Old Boultinghouse Place, which is a couple of miles east of the Smithwick Cemetery and a quarter of a mile east of Balcones Springs Camp.

Remnants of the old house and fireplaces can still be seen along RR 1431. The house, not large at all for a family of that size, was comprised of 2 halves. One side had the kitchen (some cooking was done outside, too) and a dining area, but also doubled as a sleeping area. The other side was the bedroom. The way I remember it, there was just one big room but accommodated several beds and room for pallets on the floor as well. Each side had a large fireplace. Between the two rooms was an open breezeway, or a dog run as it was called. During seasons that allowed for it, beds, cots and pallets would be brought out there to catch a breeze when there was one.

The place was comprised of 303 acres. They raised livestock and fowl as well as areas for growing crops. Besides eating what they raised on the land, they hunted and fished. Game of all types was plentiful. The Colorado River was only a mile or so from the house and there were a lot of catfish caught.

Up the creek from the house under a huge grove of oak trees was Delbert's sorghum molasses mill. People from all around who raised cane and sweet sorghum would bring it there to be pressed and the juices cooked to make syrup and molasses. The press was turned using horses or mules traveling around and around in a circle attached to long pole which extended from the center of the mill. Fires were built and huge iron pots were suspended above to cook the juices.

There was an abundance of cedar in that area, which was used for fence posts and other building needs. The Boultinghouse men were all involved in the chopping of cedar right up until WW 2 began. Back during the Depression Era, when times got very hard, Grandpa Delbert took a job up in Arkansas to make ends meet. He was working in a sawmill when he had an accident. The result was the loss of a leg. Upon returning home his health was never much good. He passed away when his youngest daughter was but 4 years old. Most of the girls were still at home and the War was going on so, times were hard, to say the least.

Grandma Nancy was a hardworking old gal and always had a positive outlook. She stayed there on the place for several more years, with family members that were away sending money to help, and a great deal of perseverance.

Around the late 40's she and the younger girls

moved to Austin where she got a job cooking at the State Hospital at Guadalupe & 38th St. Grandma continued to work and live in central Austin until the girls were all married off a decade or so later. After that she came to live with us near Jollyville Tx for several years until we all returned to Smithwick in 1964. She spent time with her kids with extended visits to California & Texas until she passed away in 1972.

~~~~~~~~~~

Charlie & Minnie Campbell – A Love Story

This story doesn't involve actual family members. It does include the Smithwick Cemetery and a couple that were a part of the community for a few years. One day Minnie and Charlie showed up in an old Studebaker car. Everything they owned was in that car. When people said their name, they always left off the p and b. It was Charlie and Minnie Camel.

They never had children and claimed they had no other close family. They just had each other. Minnie was from Oklahoma and always said she was part Indian. While she had a round pie plate face, she did have real high cheek bones. A sure sign of Indian blood, I guess.

It was probably around 1963, Charlie and Minnie were familiar to many of the older people around Smithwick. They had appeared the same way back in the 40's when they had camped out down along the river and started out this stay also by camping out. Charlie was a rock mason by trade. Minnie was his helper. He was hired to do some jobs around the community by various ones, but mostly by Cecil Lewis, my dad. My Grandfather died in the fall of 1958, so the old Lewis home place had been left vacant for several years and soon the old house became home to the Campbell's.

It was always known that Charlie was much older than Minnie. When I looked up Minnie's grave I was shocked that she was only 63 when she died. (I will turn 63 next August.) There are question marks by dates associated to Charlie on the Find-A-Grave website. No one really ever knew how old Charlie was. Camping out most of their lives, as well as the hard work of laying rock, made Minnie look much older than she was. Her skin was as leathery as a riding saddle. Charlie was well into his 80's by the time they made their second arrival to Smithwick. Upon his death in 1975 he was claiming to be 95. But who knows, Charlie claimed to be 89 when they got to Smithwick in 63.

As a young boy I enjoyed visiting with them. They

had tales to tell. Charlie was an inventor. He claimed to have invented the racks with the little clips that stores and bars hung up bags of chips and peanuts on. Someone paid him a few bucks with a promise of more, but it never came. Or at least that was Charlie's story. Minnie always agreed with everything Charlie said.

His greatest invention was a wooden level (he used levels a lot in the masonry trade.) It had a needle in the center dial instead of a bubble. While now it doesn't seem that high tech, at that time his prototype was very well put together. He had even worked with a jeweler to help balance the mechanism and fashion a dial that read out in degrees. Minnie wasn't the finest seamstress but she had sewn a velvet bag that he kept the level in. Charlie had met with several companies who were interested in buying it, but he would only tell them about it and not show it, for fear they would steal his idea. He was always trying to save up enough mo-ney to pat-ent it, but that never happened. I wish I knew what happened to the level.

Charlie chewed tobacco, but not like anyone else did. He sent off money to a cigar company in South Carolina and a few weeks later a big box would arrive with cigar clippings. Actually the box would be full of pieces of tobacco leaves. He said it was much better than what you could buy at the store. I suspected it was more about price than taste.

Minnie dipped Copenhagen snuff. That was a finely ground tobacco, and I do mean finely ground; more like tobacco dust. This was a fashionable thing for ladies to do many years ago. They would take a small spoon and place some in their lower lip and hold it there for long periods of time. Some would cut small peach tree branches a few inches long and chew on one end until it frayed, then dip it in the snuff jar and suck on it. With Minnie, she would sometimes snort the Copenhagen up her nose. That was always done discreetly. I guess it wasn't very lady like to be a snorter.

After they had been around for a couple of years, Minnie up and died. We were living in Jollyville at that time, but came directly upon getting the phone call. It was an hour's drive, but when we got there the funeral home still hadn't carried her away. Her passing became a Smithwick happening that evening. Seems like the whole community was there at the old house by the time we arrived. I remember it being really cold. Everyone mostly stood outside with heavy coats on.

After Minnie was transported away and the crowds left, it fell to Jimmy, (a local kid and old friend)

Kenny, and me, to spend the night with Charlie. Our ages were 13, 13, & 10, I was the youngest. The old house only had a fireplace for heat so they had a roaring fire going. Charlie sat for what seemed like hours that night telling the three of us about his and Minnie's life together. Much more information than we needed I'm sure.

Minnie hadn't been the most immaculate house keeper. There were always dogs, chickens and goats roaming freely in and out of the house. As the night wore on we became tired and decided to sleep in the only bed that Minnie hadn't just been lying dead in. It was a little Hollywood bed; best described as a small day bed no bigger than a twin. I think the dogs generally slept there. It was located in the corner of Minnie and Charlie's bedroom, which was far enough away that no heat was felt from the fireplace.

We found some heavy blankets and all three of us boys crawled in bed together with our clothes and shoes on. The only light was the glow of fireplace. Our Dad, Cecil, had told us to find Charlie's little 22 single shot rifle and hide it, so it was in the bed with us. I guess he was afraid Minnie's death would be too much for Charlie to take.

Charlie never went to bed that night. He sat in his wooden rocking chair by the fire. He would sob and let out loud moans, followed by extended periods of saying chants. I don't think the three of us got much sleep either. It marked the longest night of my life.

In preparation for the burial, several local men decided to dig the grave to help Charlie with funeral expenses. So on that cold day a bunch of us gathered and dug that grave, everyone taking turns. Minnie was laid to rest and Charlie was off to the next chapter in his life.

He never really adjusted completely to losing Minnie. He stayed on for a while but eventually took up residence down in Cedar Park where an old friend of his owned the Sunset Tavern. Buck (last name escapes me) was his name. There was a little room in the back for him to stay. He swept the floors, carried out the trash and waited for someone to come in and buy him beers.

He was there for a few years. I would go by to see him when I got down that way. One day I went by and the place was closed down. No way to know what happened to Charlie. Then a bit later, quite by accident, I saw Charlie walking the highway headed south on Lamar way out in north Austin. I stopped and gathered up my old friend. He said he was headed up to his girlfriend's bar.

A place called Dixie's was located at what is now Braker Ln and North Lamar. It set back off the street a ways under huge oak trees. It was just across the street from the very famous, in its time, Skyline Dance Hall on North Lamar.

He lived in some little tourist courts (tourist courts were the precursor of motels) about a mile north of that Braker Lane location. It was a series of small stone buildings that were converted into one room living units containing a bed, a counter holding a hotplate, and a small loud refrigerator. The toilet was walled of in a corner. The solid rock walls caused the place to always feel cellar like, with a damp musty smell. The place was called the Coxville Courts. (Named for a little settlement on the north end of Austin.) There was even a zoo across the street; the Coxville Zoo.

When I made my way out north I'd stop by to check on Charlie either finding him in his room, or at Dixie's. This would have been around 1975. Then my work had me out of town for several months and I didn't see Charlie. One day I got a call from my Dad that he had been contacted about Charlie's death. Dixie and Charlie had been in a traffic accident leaving him dead. I can't remember for sure but I think they both were killed.

Travis County didn't know who to contact about the death, so the body stayed at the morgue for a couple of months. Just as they were ready to bury him in the county pauper's cemetery, a Travis Co. investigator found some old mail in his room with the Marble Falls address on it. That's how they found my Dad.

They brought Charlie to Smithwick to be buried alongside the love of his life. The picture of the headstone, while it really doesn't look like much, symbolizes who Charlie and Minnie were, and how their existence was meager and simple.

~~~~~~~~~~

Trust in a Marriage

To say we married young is an understatement. We each turned nineteen in August of 1971 and were married in November of that year. We spent every day we possibly could together. We liked each other that much. She was living in Austin with a couple of gals and felt like she was working a dead-end job. She had worked at DPS at one point, but was working at Retail Merchants a credit reporting firm just prior to us marrying.

I was doing construction work in Burnet, Texas at the time. Every Wednesday I would make the hour and a half drive from Burnet to far south Austin, so I could take her out to dinner. Our favorite places to go were El Matt's Mexican restaurant at 5th and I-35, or Christie's Seafood along Town Lake, just south of the river on S. First Street. Dixie was one of her roommates that we'd grown up with in Marble Falls and would usually go with us. Most of the time we would leave the restaurant and head to the Dairy Queen on South Lamar to have a parfait.

One day we were talking about how we needed to take our relationship to the next level, so on that one particular Wednesday night we went down on Congress Ave. to Kruger Jewelers and picked out rings. David Kruger was a young man at that time, I'm sure he was either fresh out of college or perhaps still going to school and working at the family business in his spare time.

After going to pick up the rings on the following Friday evening we got back to her place and I'm sure my proposal was awkward. I don't remember exactly how it went, but most likely it was, "Here's your ring – you want to get married?" Of course I figured she did or we wouldn't have just been out buying wedding rings two days before. That was Oct. 1st.

A short engagement was planned with a January wedding. The last week of October we found out that Madeline's Dad had taken a job in Rocksprings, Wyoming and was to leave shortly. Not wanting him to have to come back to Texas so soon after leaving we decided to up the wedding date. We were married the next weekend on November the 6th. It wasn't a huge affair but it was attended by quite a few people. She and her Mother were very busy that week... I guess that's putting it mildly.

I felt confident that we could marry, live in Marble Falls, and do alright on my $3.75 an hour wage. I worked a lot of hours, so my take home pay was usually around $150 per week. Madeline had a couple of jobs early on, at Montgomery Wards in Marble Falls for a little while and then at a Day Care down in Los Escondido's that I can't remember the name. It was run by a couple, Bob and Sue Tindell. Bob was blind. I always thought it was a strange place for a Day Care, run by a blind man, since it set right up above Lake Marble Falls, high on a rock bluff.

There is more to our early married life and departure from Marble Falls, but that will have to wait for another time. Fast forward a few years to 1978. I had started my construction business in June 1972, Matthew was born in 1974 and Michael in 1977. We were buying our first real home (had been doing the mobile home thing up until then) it was located in far south Austin.

I came home one afternoon and she was in the

back end of the house. Her purse was sitting on the kitchen counter. The savings passbook was right on top. She handled all of our personal finances, but out of curiosity, I glanced to see what our current balance was. I saw where she had that day transferred money to our checking account. About then I remembered that I had forgotten something in my pickup, so I went back out to retrieve it.

As I came back inside, my lovely wife greeted me as if I was just getting home. After a few minutes, in a questioning voice I ask her why she took money from the savings account that day. It really didn't matter to me, as she was in complete control of our finances. I was just jerking her chain, just a way to mess with her. She explained that she was running short in her checking account and needed it to make ends meet. Puzzled, she asked how I knew about the withdrawal. I told her that I had a deal with the banker to call me if she ever started withdrawing money from our savings account. The subject dropped right there and we continued on with our life. I really meant to tell her the truth later that evening but it slipped my mind.

Several months later, Madeline asked if the banker had called me that day. I didn't have a clue why the banker would be calling me so I ask her what she was talking about. She reminded me of the discussion we had a few months prior and it finally started to sink in. I felt horrible after I realized what must have been going on in her head all that time. I think she forgave me. That is one reason she is so special to me. She has overlooked so much of my crap in our marriage. Madeline I love you.

The Army Draft

At the risk of sounding unpatriotic I'll tell this story anyway. The Vietnam War was a mess that seemed to be coming to an end, or at least needing to. Never the less, the draft was still very active. Kenny had been drafted a couple of years before.

It was the summer that I turned 20. My draft notice arrived. Madeline and I had married the previous November. I was already in the utility contracting business. By then I had about a half dozen employees I felt responsible for and equipment payments to make. I just couldn't see spending a couple of years in the Army. Besides, almost any-one in college was getting deferments that kept them from having to go.

A few months earlier I had crushed the bones in my left foot with a backhoe outrigger and was treated by Dr. Allen at the Allen Clinic Hospital in Burnet. I reasoned that if I went to Dr. Allen and explained my circumstance maybe he could write a letter for me. Coincidently we had just finished laying a new water main in front of his house and had visited with him. He seemed proud for me, being in business so young making my mark on the world. When I ask him for the favor he was more than happy to oblige.

The day before leaving on a bus for Abilene to get my physical, I stopped by and he had the letter ready for me. He had written that in his belief I would not be a good candidate for marching and other medical language all sounded like I may actually be crippled for life. He asked me to stop in when I returned and let him know how it went.

Not wanting to leave anything to chance I thought it would even be better if my foot was swollen a bit when I showed up in Abilene. With Big Jimmy Palmer holding me and Glenn Lewis in the pickup the plan was for him to drive over my foot. Except when Glenn felt the pickup ease up on my foot he thought it was a good idea to stop and get out and wait a little while before pulling off again. I wasn't exactly prepared for how that felt.

The next morning I drove to Lampasas where the Draft Office was located and boarded a bus for Abilene. My foot showed no signs of swelling. When I got there I handed my letter to the doctor. Looking at it he said, "That's a good ole doctor you have there."

I was told to go sit on a bench by myself. The rest of the busload was taken back, stripped naked, probed, prodded, and who knows what else. I just sat there on the bench. At the end of the day I was given my paperwork stamped 4F, meaning I was unfit for military duty.

Upon returning I stopped in to see Dr. Allen at the hospital. He was busy and told me to go back and wait in his office. He came in after he was finished seeing a patient and asked me how it went. I proudly showed him my 4F. He said, "I figured you'd be alright," then pointed to a framed certificate on the wall.

I got up and looked. It was showing him being named as Chairman of the Oversight Board of Army Medical Examiners. Sometimes it's who you know in life. In this case there is no way I would have had the nerve to approach him, had I known about his Army connection.

Since I never served it makes me that much prouder of the 3 sons and a grandson that did step up.

~~~~~~~~~~

From A Special Wall in Our Home in Bertram:

Top Row: Cecil Lewis (Dad)
Kenneth Lewis (Brother)
Theodore Jordan (Father in Law)
Bottom Row: Ron Lewis Jr. (Son)
Justin Lewis (Son)
Jason Lewis (Son)
Tyler Lewis (Grandson)

~~~~~~~~~~

The Fire

Ruby Waggoner was my dad's mother. She and my grandfather had divorced when Cecil was very young. He was raised by his dad, Theron and a host of aunts, uncles, and his grandparents. Ruby Lee, Grannie Ruby, or Grannie was a big part of our life growing up.

She lived in Austin and visited often. She was one funny old gal who laughed a lot and made the rest of us laugh. After I was grownup and had projects around north Austin, I'd stop by to see her even if for just a few minutes.

One day she and I made a plan for me to pick her up for a visit to Smithwick. I was going that way know-ing I had to return in a couple of days and could bring her back home. She was well into her eighties by then and was no longer able to drive, her eyesight being pretty well gone. This was a good chance for her to spend a couple of days with Bonnie & Cecil.

This happened in 1985. I had a project laying a wastewater line up the middle of Shoal Creek in North Austin. This wasn't far from where Grannie lived, so about midafternoon I left the crew working and drove down to picked her up. As we left her house I told her we would drive back by my job to check on things before we headed to Smithwick. She always liked to go with me to see the big machines. She had grown up on a farm and was very mechanically minded truly understanding how things worked. She and her second husband had farmed a piece of ground along Onion Creek just south of Austin.

After leaving her house we drove up a ways and as I turned on the street to go by the project I could see emergency vehicles everywhere. The job-site was right beside channel 24, the ABC affiliate's studio. The news cameras where running, gathering a good story for the evening news. As I got closer I saw that a big excavator had caught fire. I could see the operator standing out from it and he appeared to be doing okay, so I just drove on past and headed for Smithwick.

About 15 miles down the road Grannie Ruby said, "Ron, I thought you said we were going by your job?" To which I replied, "We did." Nothing else was said for several minutes then she asked, "Ron that was your job where that machine was a blazing wasn't it?" I answered, "Yes Grannie it was." Sometime later, with concern, she said, "Ron, don't you think you should have stopped to make sure everyone was alright." All I said was, "It didn't look like anyone was hurt and I didn't figure I needed to be on the six o'clock news."

After dropping her off, she told my parents she really didn't know about me. She thought maybe I should have been at least a little more concerned about things. When they called to tell me what she had said I told them to watch the 24 news to get the full story.

As it turned out, a hydraulic oil line had burst next to the exhaust manifold and that was the end of that 100,000 lb hunk of iron. And no one was injured. It was insured and I got more for the machine than it was probably worth.

~~~~~~~~~~

Granny Ruby and the Phone Call

One time around midnight Granny Ruby received a phone call. The person on the other end told her he was with the phone company and there was an indication that something was wrong in her phone and was causing a problem at the switchboard. He explained that sometimes that would happen and it needed immediate attention... with her help it could be remedied. Would she be willing to help? Being the good and helpful person she prided herself in being she said, "Sure I'll help!"

The fellow asks if her phone cord ran down to a little box by the baseboard. "Well yes it does.." she replied. (99.9% of phones did in those days.) "Good, what happens is when the installers put the phones in they get lazy and instead of cutting the wires off they'll wad up all the extra and sooner or later it will start to short out. So here's what I need you to do. Just take the cord and give it a little tug..." to which she did. "Oh, perfect this warning light went off. Looks like it's all fixed...Oh wait, its back on. It's more serious than I thought. That must mean it's really tangled up in there. Here's what I need you to do. Since its being stubborn I need you to just lay the phone down and grab the wire with both hand and pull just as hard as you can."

She followed his instructions exactly. Next thing she knew she was standing there holding the wires she'd just completely jerked out of the wall. Realizing what she had just done she imagined that is was a burglar that pulled that trick on her so he could break in and rob her and she wouldn't be able to call for the cops. She said she lay there all night afraid to even close her eyes.

The next day she went next door to call the phone company to come repair her broken phone wire. They told her they had been getting a lot of those calls lately. It was the prank that was going around at that time.

~~~~~~~~~~

The Garage Sale

I have always enjoyed playing a practical joke on people, but no one as much as my Grannie Ruby. She was always humorous and would easily laugh at herself.

With a project down in Houston going on Madeline and I had temporarily left Austin, sometimes returning on the weekends. This one weekend when we were in my sis-in-law Karen told me that Grannie Ruby was having a garage sale and she going to be taking stuff over to sell also.

Early the next morning, when I figured she had moved everything out tagged and ready, I called her up. When she answered, I disguised my voice and said I was Sgt. Joe Smith with the Austin Police Dept. I explained to her that there was a new city ordinance that didn't allow garage sales without a permit and a fee being paid.

I told her I had just driven down her street and saw that she was in violation and she had to get everything picked up out of that yard and back in the house in the next 30 minutes before I made another round. If she didn't comply, I'd handcuff her and she would be hauled off to jail.

A few minutes later as she was dragging everything back inside, Karen drove up and asked her what was happening. Upon telling of the courtesy call she had received, Karen assured her that there was no such ordinance and someone was playing a joke on her. Then Karen recalled telling me about the yard sale. A few minutes later my phone was ringing with an old woman on the other end laughing so hard she could barely talk.

Later when Madeline found out about what I'd done she wasn't very pleased at all with me. I told her I wouldn't do it again.

~~~~~~~~~~

Winfield Scott

Winfield was a grade ahead of me at Marble Falls High School. He had the reputation of doing wild and crazy things. We ran around together some, but weren't constant companions in our school days. He was extremely intelligent, but lacking in the common sense department. After high school, he went off to college and became a C.P.A.

I saw very little of Winfield throughout the 70's, as he was in Houston carving out his niche in the world of accounting. Sometime in the early 80's, I found out that he was in Austin working for a small local CPA firm. We managed to get together a few times for lunch. It seemed like Winfield's craziness had leveled off with the responsibilities of his work and by that time he had become a father. His marriage had failed, but he was able to see his daughter often and was always so happy when she was with him.

With my business growing I thought that the perfect situation was for him to join my construction company as our accountant and to oversee the financial end of our business. I made him a generous offer. He was growing tired of the humdrum of working in an accounting office and felt that my offer would give him the challenges he was looking for.

He really caught on to the business in a hurry and immediately began organizing, hiring office help, and making my life much easier. Being recently divorced he was feeling his oats and had a new story to tell about his love life daily. He kept all the guys entertained. One of the first things he did was buy a shiny red Corvette and began to get speeding tickets on a regular basis. It began to occur to me that all of his craziness hadn't completely left him. But as long as he did his job, I didn't get too excited. I often won-dered how a guy could continue to rack up all those tickets and keep his driver's license.

One day when I posed that question to him, he said his license had been revoked for a few weeks. He jokingly said now when he got stopped, he would just tell the cop that he had lost his billfold. He would then give them my name and recite my driver's license number. He had all my information memor-ized; we were approximately the same size, so that always worked. I thought he was joking at first, but after thinking about it, I knew it was a strong possibility he was telling me the truth.

A few weeks later while driving in downtown Austin, he was involved in an accident right beside the police station. It was discovered that he had several outstanding tickets and off to jail he went. Without money to bail himself out he called me with desperation in his voice, "Please bring $950 and come to the city jail and get me out." After some contemplating, I made a withdrawal and went downtown.

They had him in a holding area at the jail and when I entered I could tell he was shaken. I ask the desk sergeant if I could speak to him in private. He allowed us to go out into an adjacent hallway. I told Winfield that the only way I would get him out is if he would go confess and tell the officer he had been using my name and had racked up several tickets in my name also. If he didn't get it all straightened out I was leaving and he was going to stay. Reluctantly on Winfield's part, we returned to the booking room where he started explaining to the police sergeant what he had done.

The police sergeant was so astonished with what he was being told to him, by a Certified Public Accountant no less that he just sat there shaking his head. After Winfield had finished his story the cop left the room for a few minutes. Upon returning, he told me that my driving record had been cleared up. We were led to the pay window where they took the $950 in settlement of the outstanding tickets and allowed my C.P.A. friend to leave with me. I watched my driving record after that and never did have a problem from it.

~~~~~~~~~~

Winfield and the Wimberley Bank

I thought that the incident with Winfield and the tickets had taught him a lesson. I found out later how clueless I was about what all was going on in that man's head. If you sat and listened to him you would really take him to be just a big talker, but you also knew he wanted to make it big one day.

He had been around a couple of years by this time and my business was going through a very tumultuous time. All my bills were behind, creditors were beating our door down and Winfield was spending most of his time putting out fires. He was arranging loans for us left and right. It seemed that he always made everything workout, so we could   continue to operate. I was working on a project down near San Antonio and was away from the office most of the time. Kenny was taking care of the work in and around Austin and helping to keep an eye on Winfield.

One day Kenny called and said, "We need to talk when you get back to Austin." When I returned he told me of an incident that had taken place that week. Kenny and Winfield were the only two at the office that particular day. All the girls that Winfield had hired had long ago been sent down the road. Two men dressed in suits walked in and asked to talk to Winfield in private. Kenny figured it was someone Winfield had a deal working with. He later found out that Winfield had never laid eyes on them before, nor was he expecting them. The three of them went into my private office, the only completely private place, and shut the door. After 20 or 30 minutes they all came out and the two men left.

Nothing was said for a couple of minutes and Winfield seemed to be completely cool about everything. He then asked Kenny to come out in the backyard area as he had something to tell him. Winfield didn't want to talk inside the office, for fear it was bugged. The two men were FBI Agents. After walking out back, Winfield's knees began to wobble and he could barely speak. Outside in the open yard he felt it safe to tell Kenny the following story.

Winfield had moved back home with his folks in Marble Falls and almost every evening after work he would stop and get drunk at a little beer joint up near the Pedernales River. He and a drinking buddy, an ex-Vietnam Marine, had started discussing how easy it would be to rob a bank. They figured a sleepy little place like Wimberley, Texas would be a perfect place to pull it off.

In a lot of ways Wimberly was a town and had all the businesses you associate with a town. Many people vacationed there and a big housing development had brought retirees to the area. It just didn't have a government; therefore it didn't have a police force. The Hays County Sherriff's Dept. was the law enforcement authority but was headquartered some 25 miles away. That made it the perfect place to rob.

After some planning they decided that a third person would be needed. The Marine had a buddy who had served in Vietnam with him and would be perfect for the job. But after a meeting or two the number three guy began to get cold feet, yet never mentioned it. He fell out of sight, but they thought he would reappear by the time of the heist. He wasn't really needed for the planning anyway.

Number three guy went to the FBI. Now with the authorities in on their plan, they were constantly being watched. The two suits who came to the office that day had told Winfield every move he had made and every person he had called for the past couple of weeks. They had followed Winfield and the Marine as they staked out the Wimberley Bank on two occasions. (I would find out later they had gone in one of my company trucks.) The FBI Agents warned Winfield that if he decided to act out any more of this fantasy, he would regret it. It seems strange that he wasn't arrested. They also warned him about retaliating against the informant. I never knew if they spoke with Winfield's accomplice. I suspect they did. As far as I know all plans of robbing banks for Winfield died that day. Winfield went on to become Personal Injury Lawyer in Houston. I always wondered if he was ever nervous about his past as he studied to become an attorney and whether he would be certified. I guess there was nothing in his record about the incident.

Winfield did live to do many more outrageous things before he was found dead in 1995 of a drug overdose, or a slaying over a drug deal gone badly. All this was going on while Winfield was dealing with banks on my behalf. I'm sure my bankers would have been impressed if Winfield, my CPA had been arrested for bank robbery.

~~~~~~~~~~~

MQ Scott and the Hog Buyer

This story was told to me by Winfield about his Dad, MQ Scott. I'm pretty sure that MQ was as crazy as his son, Winfield. There are many stories about him but none that top the following. I had only limited contact with him when I was a kid. The first time I remember seeing MQ was during a hog buying episode when he bought a pen full of hogs from Brown Parker. As we loaded the hogs something happened that caused MQ to slip down in the loading chute with a big sow on top of him. He literally bit her ear; then once he was up on his feet he started beating her in the head with his fists and screaming. Then he lit into Winfield for no reason that anyone there could explain. The encounter ended with Brown and Cec running him off telling to never come back on our place again. I don't think he ever did.

Now the True-to-Form MQ story Winfield told me:

A hog buyer from Arkansas came to the Scott Hog Farm and bought a truck (big cattle truck size) load of hogs and paid MQ with a check. The buyer and the hogs went to Arkansas. The check bounced.

The buyer showed up wanting more hogs. MQ asked about the hot check, not wanting to get stuck for a second load. A deal was made for a second load under the condition that he would be paid with certified funds for both. The truck was loaded and told to follow them to the Big Wheel Truck Stop in Oak Hill in the edge of Austin. The driver was to sit and wait. MQ drove the hog buyer downtown to one of the big banks where the guy had made arrangements to get a certified check for both loads. The buyer directed MQ to pull up to a walk-up window at 8th and Guadalupe where he has been told that a check would be waiting. In a matter of minutes there were Austin PD cars with lights flashing and sirens blaring coming from every direction. The buyer had walked up to the window, handed the teller a note saying the guy in the brown Ford LTD had kidnapped him and was going to kill him if he didn't pay a ransom. Once the cops starting arriving the buyer faded away into the hustle-bustle of downtown Austin, supposedly meet-ing up with the truck and headed out for Ark-ansas.

By the time MQ was arrested, booked into jail, and allowed to tell his version of events, the guy was long gone, never be heard from again. The real pro-blem was there was no evidence of who the guy was or where he was actually from. The check had been a complete forgery.

~~~~~~~~~

Winfield and the Farming Enterprise

When Winfield left Austin on shaky ground with me, and many others may I add, he ended up in Oklahoma for a short time. Doing what? Trying to go into the Utilities Construction business. That venture didn't make it far, but I wasn't surprised. One day when he was coming through Austin from Oklahoma he called and wanted to stop for a visit. We agreed to meet at one of my jobsites. I had just purchased a microcassette recorder and was playing with it when Winfield drove up. Knowing that I was going to hear some wild stories that I may want to share with Kenny and others I pushed the record button and laid it down on the seat as Winfield got in.

Of course, in typical Winfield fashion he told me about his recent conquests. Just guy talk. Then he launched into his plans for a new business venture. He was going to start a farming business. When I asked what he would be growing, he would never say. Since it was Winfield I knew what it was. He assured me he the perfect area picked out and all the components in place to become quite wealthy.

A couple of weeks later I heard from a friend in Marble Falls that the whole Scott family had been arrested; minus Winfield. His mother, dad and brother were at home at Double Horn when the raid came down. The tax appraiser had been to the Scott place looking around when he peered through a garage window to see the whole thing filled with potted marijuana plants ready to be set out.

I called Winfield to inquire. He thought I was kidding; I assured him I wasn't. I could imagine the blood draining out of his face as we talked. His voice quaked and I knew he was shaken. Winfield mostly fell out of sight for a while. I would get a call from him occasionally asking me to call his mom, Mrs. Scott and let her know he was alright. When there was a court date coming up, she would call and ask me to let Winfield know. It occurred to me one day that I was in the middle of one of the craziest stories to ever come out of Burnet County. I'm not sure exactly how the case was disposed of, but it seems like most charges got dismissed with the Scott's not having to serve time beyond that at the initial arrest.

After things settled down when I would talk to Winfield I'd play the tape that was made when he first talked about farming. I think there was even a price established for me to turn the tape over, but I never saw the money. I think I still have it somewhere.

~~~~~~~~~

The Funeral

I should let this story be the final one for Winfield, but I will go ahead and tell it now, because there are many other Winfield chapters between the ones I wrote earlier and the end. I'm sure a lot of people wondered what ever happened to him.

His family was pretty well off in terms of most of us. His dad had a good job at one of the dams in the area and also had the large hog farm. Winfield left Marble Falls in a Porsche headed to LSU in the fall of 1969. Like I mentioned he became a CPA then went to work in Houston for one of the big national firms. He aced all parts of the CPA exam which I'm told is very hard to do. Winfield had a fantastic memory and very seldom studied for anything.

After several years as a CPA and working for me, he decided to study law and by the early 1990's Winfield had finished law school and went on to become a successful attorney doing personal injury law in Houston. We remained friends and kept in touch during those years talking often on the phone. Things were wonderful for a time for him. He made a lot of money.

Houston was a bad place to be if you had a lot of money and were single. The party life began to take a toll on him. The alcohol was bad but the cocaine was his real problem. Cocaine was everywhere in Houston in the 90's. I got a call from him one day in 1993 I believe. He told me he was no longer interested in being an attorney. I later found out the he had been disbarred for cocaine possession. He was really in denial about his circumstances.

The new Winfield was moving on to become a Goat Rancher. The Valley, as it is called, is in the far south part of Texas and has a large Hispanic population and the need for meat goats. Cabrito was a real burgeoning market. At his old law firm in Houston he had become involved with a gal who had family ties to the Valley and through that connection he could sell as many goats as he could find. This was Winfield's new meal ticket. He enlisted my help finding anyone with meat goats for sale. I never referred him to any goat raisers I knew. Nothing really seemed right about anything he said. He was a mess. I really didn't want any part of him. I knew real trouble wasn't far away.

One day in May, 1995, I opened the Austin paper to the obituaries. Winfield was listed. I wasn't surprised. The funeral was that afternoon. I was already in Austin on a jobsite, so I called my wife Madeline to tell her. She brought clothes for me and we attended the graveside service held in a little community southeast of Austin where his Dad had been raise. Only a handful of people were there, perhaps 25. The only ones I recognized were his Mother, his older Brother, his Daughter, and the Ex-Wife. The remaining attendees were just local folks that had known the Scott family from years ago.

It was a somber day, rainy. A very pretty Hispanic

lady picked me out. We had never met, but she knew who I was. She was the girlfriend from the Valley. As we waited for the service to begin, she led me aside to tell me what had happened. Winfield had rented a little house out in the country south of Houston with room to pasture goats waiting to be shipped south by the truckloads. You could tell she was a believer in the goat business. She said a drug deal had gone bad and left Winfield floating in a bathtub full and overflowing with water. She seemed to know more than she told me. I wasn't surprised and I suppose it made no difference.

The service finally got under way. The casket was left open during the brief words that were spoken. That was strange to me, but everything was strange that day. Everything in Winfield's life was strange, so why was his funeral going to be any different.

Afterwards the funeral director closed the lid on the casket. His mother, accompanied by her remaining son, arose and approached the casket to place a rose on the lid. Emotions were high, for a mother burying a son they always are. As she reached out with the rose she fell across the casket hugging it. At that moment she cried out, "Oh Lord why did it have to be this One?"

Everyone was stunned, hesitant to look at each

other. A short few minutes later Madeline and I were on the road back to Austin, unsure of what had just transpired. In the years since then it is hard for me to go to a funeral without thinking of that day. Madeline and I have talked on many occasions about how bizarre that whole thing was.

A Postscript: On Feb. 12, 2010 my miniature Beagle named Jazzy ran under the rear wheel of my truck when I arrived home. She had only been in my life for about a year and a half but she had really found a place in my heart. I am not a typical dog lover, but I don't hate dogs either. I can make it fine without one in my life. We have had several different dogs over the years, each meeting death for one reason or the other. I let Jazzy get to me. She was the only dog I ever bought myself. All the others were someone else's idea.

Given the short life span of a dog compared to a person, you expect to outlive them the day you bring them home. But that was too short of a time for me and Jazzy. I was very saddened by the loss. Madeline wasn't home when it happen. The rear wheels of the truck rolled over her rear legs. I took her to our local vet. I knew it was serious. She was in real pain. I left her there for x-rays. It was only a short time before I got the call.

The damage was extensive. Not only were several bones broken but her intestines were also very messed up. The vet said she could be fixed, but healing was going to take many months and be very costly. There was no way of knowing how many complications she could have. I saw no reason for such a sweet puppy to suffer the pain she would have to endure just so I could continue to have her in my life. I decided it was best to terminate her life.

I went out under the big oak tree where several other dogs and a hamster were buried. I dug yet another hole and drove to the vet clinic to retrieve her remains. Upon returning I saw that Madeline had arrived home so I phoned to tell her I was back. She said she would come right out so we could bury her together. I placed the little lifeless body in the hole. Lucy (a mutt that had been left here by one of our sons) and I stood there at the edge looking down while Madeline walked the 50 yards from the house to the burial plot.

Just as she arrived beside us I fell to my knees and wailed, "Oh Lord why did it have to be this One?" I think my wife was as startled then as we both had been some 15 years earlier at the funeral of our friend Winfield. I looked up at her and we both broke out into a fit of laughter that lasted until the grave was filled in and we both were back inside the house.

If not for the opportunity to laugh in a moment like that, the sorrow would have been much worse with no purpose being served by it. I am giving serious thought to making my last request be that my funeral be presided over by a standup comic rather than a minister. We'll see how that plays out.

~~~~~~~~~

Selling Firewood

While it's probably evident that I enjoy talking about myself, I have a few stories to tell which were told to me along the way. This one provided a good lesson that proves that things are not always as they seem. Years ago I had an accountant working for me that previously had worked for a wealthy gentleman over in Rockdale. GK was the accountant; Pete Caulfield was his previous employer.

Mr. Caulfield was in almost any business where he could make money. In his earlier years, during the Depression, he had a little money so he hired guys to cut firewood. Being in the spring and summer he paid them to cut it and stack it in "ricks." A rick, as they termed it, was imply an orderly stack that was mea-surable, so he could figure the amount they had cut, with no guess work involve. He would return in the fall and winter time to load up the wood and take it around selling it. It all seemed simple enough.

After months spent getting his stockpiles built up, he had paid the cutters and they were long gone. Firewood season came upon the area and he went out to start loading his wood. Low and behold, in every rick of wood there was a stump. The cutters had cut a tree down and purposefully concealed the stump in the stacks of wood. As he went along every rick of wood was done the same way.

After that experience, every time he went into a business deal he would always say, "Let's look at this real carefully to be sure they haven't ricked around a stump on us." GK said that situation from years before probably had as much to do with his lifetime of success than just about any other factor.

I have used the "rick around a stump" test in many dealings myself. Some people will find a way to screw you if you let them.

~~~~~~~~~~

A Lesson in Money Collecting

Back in the late part of the 70's, we were hired by Mike O'Conner to install waterlines for several streets he developed off of Mormon Mill Rd out north of Marble Falls. He paid pretty well through-out the project, but when it came down to the end he kind of locked down and kept giving me the run around.

Knowing that he was fairly new to MF and really wanted to be respected by the townsfolk, especially the rancher types that drank coffee together every morning at the café, I thought I'd use that to my advantage. So when I met up with Ole Mike I asked him about my final money, he hummed and hawed for a good little while, but when I said, "They all told me you'd screw me out of at least part of my money..." he demanded. "WHO SAID THAT?" I replied, "Oh, all those guys down at the coffee shop..." Faster than a speeding bullet he had that checkbook out and wrote me a check, saying, "Here is your money, now go down there and tell them Mike O'Conner paid you every cent he owed you." And that I did.

~~~~~~~~~~~

Kenny-The Tiger

One day in the late 70's my brother Kenny stopped after work to have a pop or two with Don, a foreman that worked with us. It was the day of a birthday celebration (I forget whose birthday it was) at the Lewis household. It became quite late and Kenny had forgotten to come home.

As he was in no condition to drive, Don took him home, got him to the front door and rang the doorbell. Then he hurried back to his pickup before Karen answered the door. Unable to stand Kenny was found at the front door on hands and knees. "I'm a Tiger, roar....roar..." was his mantra for the night.

Karen grabbed him lovingly by the hair of the head and led the tiger into the kitchen. (Oh, let's not leave out that her parents were there that night for the party.) A freezer of homemade ice cream was still sitting there, only partially frozen by then. Not wanting The Tiger to completely miss out on party, Karen began to feed him the half thawed concoction, letting it flow down his chin to completely coat his upper body. Figuring the rest shouldn't be wasted she dumped it in his hair and massaged it in. Now the tiger was escorted off to bed.

Kenny recounted that when he woke up the next morning and attempted to raise his head from the pillow, he couldn't. He sat upright in bed with the pillow stuck to his head. The sheets gave the morning a mummified feel. Peeling the bedcovers from his body was very much like we've all seen on YouTube videos of wax hair removals. I don't think the Tiger felt so much like roaring for a day or two. But soon enough he was let out of his cage to roam another night.

~~~~~~~~~~

Glenn and the Hat

If you grew up in Marble Falls you knew Glenn. If you ever passed through Marble Falls you may have encountered Glenn. He was a real live cowboy doing ranch work most of his life. You always hear it said, "That ole boy was born a hundred years too late..." In Glenn's case there was never a truer cliché used. He was rugged, both inside and out. As a young man you seldom saw him when he wasn't riding a horse, or didn't have one in a trailer behind an old pickup. He was 5 years older than me and 3 years older than Kenny. There was a lot to be learned from Glenn.

We shared the same last name, but one has to go way back to find how we connect by blood kin. My brother Kenny and I were thrown together with Glenn often. His mother and our step-grandmother were sisters. (Leona, Maw-Maw, Aunt Nonie – you'll hear a lot more out of her. She was probably my greatest supporter and the person that made me most want to do right by others – but that's for another day.)

Throughout our upbringing, Glenn was always part of the goat gathering and shearing days I've talked about, as well as a part of many Smithwick adventures. I most fondly recall the Marble Falls Rodeo every year. That weekend we would come and spend it with Glenn bringing our horses; well most of the time I'd bring Tar Baby. From the buildup of the Friday afternoon parade right on to the Friday and Saturday night rodeo there was something exciting happening around town.

Few people I've ever run across in life who knew Glenn didn't have a story to tell. Glenn was as likely to unload a horse out of the trailer and ride it into the beer joint as he was to ride along Backbone Creek to chase down and rope a colored child just to scare them to death. I don't remember ever seeing, or hearing of him really hurting a human by roping them, but then again I wasn't always with him.

Legend has it that in the late 60's he and several other cowboys were gathering cattle down in south Texas along the Rio Grande below Eagle Pass. In the heat of the day they decided to ride across the river to a small village where they proceeded to rope the citizenry and tie some up. They took over the little cantina and were having a party when someone was able to get word to the Mexican Federales and summoned them from Eagle Pass.

Most of the cowboys were still sober enough to see what was happening and got on their horses and rode back to safety. Glenn and a couple of others weren't that sober. Luckily the rancher they were working for was well connected to Washington DC and the Mexican Government, so their stay in a Mexican Jail was limited to a few days. I loaned Glenn $500 to finish paying his way out of that mess. I guess it seemed like the thing to do at the time. He gave me the title to his old blue and white 62' model Ford pickup. Years later he needed the title so he could trade it off, so I gave it back to him.

A favorite story told by many puts him at the Circle Inn on a Saturday night. It was one of those hot summer nights that cause people to not always get along. Glenn and another patron got into a fight and the Proprietor, Alice Sayers ushered them outside. Alice wasn't someone you wanted to mess with. (I know, I married her granddaughter.)

Rather than getting in his pickup and leaving, Glenn walked to the back of the building (he had consumed huge amounts of beer) took the back off of the old-timey water cooler that blew damp cool air across the dance floor and relieved himself. The moist cool air turned to a fine mist of urine as the squirrel cage fan slung warm piss the full width of the building. Glenn wasn't in most people who were there that night's best graces for a while.

When I started my first construction project; a subcontract to lay new water mains all over Burnet, Texas in 1972, Big Jimmy Palmer and Glenn were my first two employees. They were hard workers and dependable. That summer we laid water lines and installed fire hydrants down what seemed like every street in Burnet. When I drive down those streets now, almost every block brings back a funny memory of some kind.

When we finished in Burnet we moved on to Lakeway and then other projects around Austin. Madeline and I were newly married and I had sworn off alcoholic beverages, so I didn't get involved in their night life too much. There were always wild stories every morning. You can only imagine what bringing Big Jimmy and Glenn to the big city to live for the first time was like.

The time with Glenn being away from Marble Falls came to an end after a couple of years, but Big Jimmy hung around for a few more before his lust for the nightlife took precedence over construction work. He became a bouncer and then a manager of a south Austin favorite nightspot.

Dial the clock forward to the fall of 1979. My brother had joined me in 1976 in the construction business after he finished a six year stint in the Army. We had contracted to build a nice housing subdivision on RR 2222 in west Austin, The Cliff's Over Lake Austin. Kenny & I walked down through that heavily treed piece of property and found a wealth of straight cedar trees that was perfect for harvesting cedar posts for fence building. So rather than send a dozer through to clear we decided to put a crew of chainsaw wielding Mexicans together to maximize our profits.

Kenny ran onto Glenn in Marble Falls and struck a deal with him to come be foremen over that crew; something he was very familiar with. His job was to keep the guys lined out, the saws running, and the chains sharp. They had been working on that project a few weeks when Christmas came along. Back in those days it was customary to give all the guys a small Christmas bonus check, a frozen turkey or ham and a bottle of whiskey to celebrate the season with.

The Cliff's Over Lake Austin was a fairly central location, so we sent word that at an appointed time everyone would meet there. Kenny and our book-keeper Woody, an elderly fellow, gathered up everything we needed and I, along with about 50 guys met them there. They all pulled down inside the cleared site so everyone could have a few beers out of sight of anyone.

I was driving a new 80' Buick Riviera and didn't want to scratch it up so I stopped alongside of the highway and walked down a path to join the others. We stood around, everyone visiting with chainsaws still running far off in the background when Kenny walked to the back door of his pickup and retrieved a big box. It was my Christmas present that all of the employees had gone together to buy.

In the box was a beautiful 100X beaver cowboy hat. That is the best quality hat known to man. Even that long ago, it still cost around $500. I proudly removed it from the box with its perfect crease and shape and put it on my head. Every man in attendance couldn't have been prouder. With the sound of the saws going silent, Glenn and the guys came up out of the brush to join us. Glenn was mostly unknown to all the other hands as he had been hired and put on that project away from all the others.

As Glenn walked up he started admiring the new hat. He knew a good hat when he saw one; the thinner the brim on a hat the better the quality. The brim on this hat was almost paper thin. When he said, "Here let me see it!" I answered; "No way!" because his hands were covered with filthy grim from working on chain saws all day. He walked over to a truck and got some go-jo hand cleaner and carefully cleaned his hands using water from a drinking can.

Seeing his hands were clean I handed him the hat. He turned it this way and that way admiring it. He still didn't know that I had been given the hat by my loyal employees. Suddenly he started wadding up the hat, rolling it in against his oily dirty jacket that covered his belly. Within seconds the hat became a ruined mess. Everyone was stunned, especially me. I grabbed the hat from him and stormed out of there in a huff, getting in my fine automobile and left.

A couple of miles down the road something exploded inside me. I turned around and headed back. As if it were in a movie, me driving as fast as I could going back, I hit the shoulder of the road, locked up my brakes and slid right up to where I'd been previously parked. Kenny & Glenn at the same moment appeared out of the brush with many of the others behind them.

In a huge cloud of dust I flung my door open, stepped out and immediately grabbed onto the back of Glenn's big heavy denim jacket, pulling it up over his head and locking his arms in a fully upward position. He was helpless to move. One hand tightly holding onto the jacket, the other made into a tight fist I went to work on his face, completely transforming it. That lasted for a short while, with him finally tripping me up (at the time he would go 260 lbs. to my 165 lbs) we tumbled to the ground. At that point Kenny and others stepped in to separate us. I'll always remember how Glenn's face resembled a package of raw hamburger meat more than it did a human being.

With my shirt torn almost completely off, I headed across town to home. It was the evening we were hosting a Christmas Party for Madeline's family. When I arrived they were all there, even Alice Sayers. All I had to do was tell them it was something Glenn Lewis was involved in.

Glenn left that day and didn't return. He really wouldn't have been welcomed back. We didn't speak again for a few years. Soon afterward he married, took a job on the Arrowhead Ranch, and lived out the rest of his life without nearly as much calamity.

One day a few years later I passed by where he was building fence along a highway. Seeing him I turned around and went back. We stood on the side of road for a long while recalling the many different memories we had. We visited many other times until his passing in early 2012, each time jokingly the hat incident was brought up.

I'll never know whether that afternoon on the side of RR 2222 changed him, or getting married did it. I suspect it was some of both, but he undoubtedly was a changed man for the last half of his life.

Footnote: Kenny sent the hat off to the Resitol Factory for me. They cleaned, blocked, and made it look completely new. That, my friends, is why good quality hats are well worth the money.

~~~~~~~~~~

The Double Tailed Quarters

There was a time in the 80's when things were really good in the construction business. I was flying high, as was Kenny and our friend Coy. We all had our own businesses but worked together at times, hiring each other's companies to help out on projects.

Kenny & Coy had a lot more in common with each other than with me. During that phase of their lives they each were without the benefit of a wife at the time, or at least they acted like it. They worked hard and partied hard as the old saying goes. Now me, I was mostly a home body, not wanting to even think about how much child support for 5 boys might cost, I was home every night.

I ate lunch with the guys almost daily and that, like everything else, always turned into a game of chance. We all 3 would get a quarter out and simultaneously flip it in the air and palm it. When showing it, the odd man would be the one to buy. We did that for a long time when one day I was visiting with Madeline's grandfather, Pops. He was a very accomplished machinist. I got him to shave the faces off four quarters, leaving each $\frac{1}{2}$ the original thickness. I then super glued them together to produce two quarters with tails on both sides.

I guess because I was thinking back to the hay hauling days or some other times that I may have not been treated fairly by my brother, I picked Coy as my accomplice. So from that moment on if we had coffee I would intentionally show a head up on another quarter so it assured that Coy, or I would lose. But when we had big juicy steaks, the special coins would always be used to insure that Kenny paid. Besides the money savings, the best part was seeing Kenny's total disgust with losing. He really doesn't like losing.

It came time for the three of us to go to Utah on a hunting trip. We rented a motorhome for the trip. Couple of thousand dollars for that... Yep Kenny lost. Filled it up with beverages and such for several hundred more dollars; nothing but the finest brands. Yep.

Sometime after we returned from the trip, which is a story unto itself, we each carelessly stuck our special quarters in a pay phone and they were gone forever. For whatever reason one day we told Kenny about the quarters. He swelled up like an old toad for a couple of days and wouldn't even play odd man out with us. Heck I don't think he would even meet us for lunch for a while. Soon things returned to normal and he only gets testy now when someone brings up the subject of the double tailed quarters.

~~~~~~~~~~

Rosalinda

John was a very good friend of mine. After the following story we have remained friends, which is surprising. We were working on a big project in the Oak Cliff area of Dallas. It was a really tough job in one of the roughest areas of one the most crime ridden cities at that time. Everything was a disaster. We tried to keep a sense of humor about it, keep the mood light, or we couldn't have endured. (More on this another day.)

We both lived back in Austin and frequently flew on Southwest out of Love Field. Many times we took the same flight, but our schedules didn't work out this one Friday with John leaving before me. The night before John and others had been out drinking and dancing with him bringing a pretty young Hispanic gal back to his apartment.

When I got to the airport on Friday, I pulled in and parked right next to John's suburban. While sitting around that weekend I composed a note to be left on John's windshield. I don't remember the exact wording but it went something like this:

"Hey señor, my name is Manual Gonzales. The beautiful lady you spent the night with last night is my wife Rosalinda. We have a fight and she left to come to Cowboys Dance Hall but I follow her. I saw when you took to your apartment. I was waiting when you dropped her off this morning. I followed you to your place of work on Kiest Blvd. I just wanted to talk to you but I couldn't get the courage. I followed you here to the Airport, but you got away before we could talk so I'm just writing you this letter.

When you return will you call me so we can meet. I promise I won't hurt you, but I just want you to assist me in getting Rosalinda to love me again. My phone number is..........."

There were billboard messages around DFW back then for Dial-A-Prayer so I used that number. I had a friend rewrite it so he wouldn't detect my hand-writing. I took a Sunday flight back so I could get an early start on Monday. After arriving back in Dallas, with the note in place I went on about my business. The next morning at the time we were expecting John to arrive at the jobsite, he didn't show up. Finally I got ahold of him by cell phone. He wasn't feeling well. He had gone to his apartment, but would be in later.

I worried that maybe I'd gone too far, driven him over the edge. Finally he got there but looked awful. I went into his office to see what was wrong. He was shaken beyond anything I had imagined. He laid it all out. Yes the whole story. After savoring the moment for a few minutes, I let him off the hook. Within seconds the color had returned to his shortly before ashen face.

~~~~~~~~~~

Death by Seatbelt

Once. when we were doing a project in Dallas, my Suburban was having mechanical problems so I took it to the shop. They gave me a rental car. This was in the early 90's. Kenny was up helping me on that project and we would go eat before going to our apartment each evening.

This night we determined where we were going, but on the way I changed my mind. He was behind me and when we stopped at a red light I opened the driver's door and stuck my head out to tell him to follow me. What I didn't realize was the shoulder belt was attached up at the top to a little moving track that carried it forward when you opened the door and then when you close it the shoulder belt would move to the back to secure you in your seat.

So when I opened the door the belt went up around my neck and when I closed the door it came back.

It had no slack in it, so there I was sitting with a green light, being choked, and at the same time pulled back tight against the seat unable to reach the door handle, which was the only way to release the belt. Kenny could tell something was wrong, me flailing around, sitting through a green light. He thought I was having a heart attack.

Finally I stretched farther than I should have been capable of and with my finger tip opened the door. With disaster averted we continued on to the restaurant and a night of laughing over the calamity that has just occurred.

~~~~~~~~~~

He Bit My Thumb

There are a few things in life that really don't mix. Being really tough and drinking too much is a good example of this. Cecil Lewis was tough guy and he drank way more than he should have. Back in 80-81 I had contracted to build a new state park and campground area down on the Guad-alupe River near the little community of Bergheim not far from Boerne, Texas. When I needed him my dad would help me out on projects. On this job he mostly drove a water truck.

He never drank while on the job that I could tell. However, one Monday morning he showed up for work and it was very apparent that he was in no condition to drive a truck, or do anything else. I wanted him off the job before anyone else saw him. I just didn't need that kind of hassle in my life. It was early in the morning and no one else was there yet. All he needed to do was load up and head out.

I left for a few minutes but when I returned he was still there. He had a good reason. As drunks sometimes do, he had left his headlights on and his battery was run down. I agreed to jump start his pickup if he would just leave. While I was hooking up the cables, he said something that I didn't agree with. He wanted me to know he could drive that truck as well as I could. We got his pickup started and rather than leave he got out and wanted to argue.

I finally got right up in his face wagging my finger. He grabbed my hand and bit down on my left thumb and wouldn't let go. A wrestling match ensued with both of us ending up on the ground. I was finally able to get back on my feet but still stooped over. When I saw that he wasn't letting go, I put one foot on his chest and stood straight up. My thumb came loose.

The pain was excruciating. I had literally skinned all the hide off my thumb. When he was once again standing on his feet, I couldn't believe what I saw. His two front teeth were sticking straight out the front of his mouth, but still attached to his gums. He then pushed them both back into place. Making a whistling sound as he spoke, he said, "Damn Ron, why did you do that?" Then he started to laugh, a drunken laugh. When he laughed, his teeth would flutter. It was comical looking, but all I could think about was both of us getting out of there.

For the next couple of days they just dangled in his mouth when he spoke. After figuring they weren't going to take new root and return to normal, he pulled them himself. He lived the last fifteen years of his life with false teeth. My thumb finally healed, but it took a while.

Madeline sees this incident as a low point for the Lewis family. She wasn't very proud of us. In fact she took it harder than either of us.

~~~~~~~~~~

The Motorola Radios

Things are so different today than when I first got into the business some 43 years ago. When people were out on a jobsite and you needed to tell them something you drove out and delivered the message in person. Austin was a much smaller place then, but a message could still be delayed several hours at times. I think we had better planning skills then, or our expectations for getting much done was a lot less.

Somewhere along the way voice pagers came into vogue. When you heard the thing buzz, while out on a job with machinery running, you grabbed it and quickly cupped it to your ear hoping to hear your message. Some had a feature where it would let you run to the truck where it was quieter and replay the message. Then, if you had time, you drove to a pay phone to return the call. Years later the digital pager came along that saved phone numbers, if the people calling were smart enough to punch in their correct number.

There was also Motorola 2 way radio's back then that big established companies used, but they were out of our price range for a long time. By about 1978 we finally got established enough to buy 2-ways and had them installed in all our pickups. We felt like we

were, for lack of a better way to say it, doing #2 in
high cotton. (If that doesn't translate for the
younger crowd, ask me next time you see me and I'll
explain it.) I need to mention, these things worked
like a party line. Maybe 8 or 10 other companies were
on with us and we all had call signs we said before we
transmitted – "WFA 407, unit 51 to unit 52" was how
we contacted each other.

It was in the fall of the year and the first really
cold spell had just blown in. We had a project that
we were doing up on Far West Blvd. Kenny was with
me and we were sitting in my pickup watching a crew
work. We were doing some boy-talk, you know like
brothers will do. We launched into a diatribe about
how good it was to be the Lewis Brothers sitting in
that pickup with the heater running, instead of being
out there freezing our assets off.

What I failed to realize was when they installed
my radio mic holder clip they put it too close to
steering column. If you hung it up with the cord
down it was fine, but if you hung it up the other way,
upside down, the mic button would be engaged. I had
hung it up the wrong way.

When it became obvious to Woody, our office
manager that all the BS being broadcast by the Lewis Boys was unfiltered and not for public consump-

tion, he panicked. He figured we were out at the new jobsite on the other side of Austin so driving there to tell us was out of the question. So he figured the base station in the office would be more powerful and would drown us out if he started talking over us.

Woody yelled into it for a while. Finally he got one of the guys with a company pickup that was in the office to go out and listen. Sure enough, with the base station mic pushed in you only heard a garbling sound. So he laid the big Austin phone book on the button and went back to work.

Sometime later during our bull session, I looked down and a little red light on the front of the radio was illuminated. That meant I was transmitting. How could that be? Then I saw why it was on and remembered how long since I'd talked and how long we had been sitting with on it. All I could think of was... "This is a very unfortunate situation that we find ourselves in."

Later, when I got to the office, Woody proceeded to lecture me on the proper use of those radios and how profanity shouldn't be used and blah blah blah. "If you and your brother keep doing that they'll revoke our license!" That may be the only time I ever raised my voice with Woody. I felt bad afterwards. Heck, I was already feeling bad when I got to the office that day.

Oh, did I mention that the vehicles all had big bullhorns installed so the men could hear them across the whole jobsites.

~~~~~~~~~~

Yet Another Motorola Situation

I was interviewing Marvin for an important position with the company and was taking him around showing him the various projects that were on going. We were driving around the city when it came over the radio that a certain truck driver had pulled yet another bone head stunt.

After having a heated conversation from my end of the radio, instead of hanging up the mic I pitched it down in the center console. At that point, making sure that Marvin could see that I was a no nonsense leader of the outfit, I went into a rant about running that driver and who knows who else off if they didn't start getting things straighten out around that company. This particle rant lasted longer than normal. I was sure than Marvin was getting the idea. Just then I noticed that the transmit light on the radio was glowing that bright red color. Upon further inspection I discovered that when I flung the radio mic down, it had went in an empty coffee cup and wedged the button open. My entire diatribe had been heard by everyone in earshot of a few dozen radios. When I got back to the office, Woody scolded me again. This time I took it like the little mouse I was that day.

~~~~~~~~~~

My Carwash Story

I had just bought a new 95 model Oldsmobile 98. The big fancy Olds. It was almost the size of an Abrams Army Tank. A recently remodeled Texaco station at Texas 29 and IH35 in Georgetown had just been reopened for business. Tyler, my first grandson was about 3 years old and went with me as often as I could take him. We stopped to fill up with gas and decided to try out the new car wash with the big whirling brushes. I figured Tyler would get a kick out of driving through that tunnel and seeing the car washed from the inside.

When we first entered everything was going fine. Suddenly a loud popping sound started that had a rhythm to it and sounded like gun shots. I could see that the windshield was broken. It had to be gunshots. By that time I had shoved Tyler into the passenger floor and I was on top of him. There really wasn't room for us both to be in that small a space. The shots were coming from the front and then from the rear. They kept going. Because I'd gotten the super duper wash we couldn't just drive out. Finally the rinse cycle started and the shooting stopped.

I can remember Tyler saying over and over... "Wat wud dat dandad, wat wud dat...?" Fearful, I didn't want to drive out, but I sure didn't want us to be sitting ducks waiting for the shooter to reload.

Then I noticed a length of garden hose dangling from the brushes. We drove forward out of the car wash. When I got out of the car I discovered that my new car didn't have many straight pieces of tin on it, the windshield was smashed and the driver's side mirror was broken out. All this due to a worker cleaning the stall had left a garden hose stretched out in the floor and the brushes had picked it up. The brass end had done the damage. Almost $5,000 worth of damage.

Of course it couldn't be as simple as the manager taking responsibility for it and giving me his insurance company name. It was my fault. Evidently I shouldn't have driven in there if a hose was left lying in the floor. Things got a little western (as they say) before he turned over the information I was requesting. Poor Tyler still may not like car washes to this day. I need to ask him.

~~~~~~~~~~

Dink Wrote Me the Check

George Lester McDuff was a fiery little fellow. Everyone called him Dink and he always had a story to tell. He had the ability to make me laugh. He could make anyone laugh. I first met Dink in 1963, when I was just a kid. He and my dad worked for the same utility construction company.

Dink ran the road boring division. Road boring is where a horizontal hole is drilled under a roadway or railroad track then pipe is installed. It was dirty work with mud knee deep and oil and grease every-where. But everyday Dink showed up in starched blue jeans, a starched white shirt with snaps rather than buttons, and wearing a pair of the most expensive of cowboy boots available. Oh, let me not forget expen-sive cowboy hats and gold. He had a proclivity to wearing a lot of gold, nugget style gold that was popular in that day. Sometimes within minutes he would have mud all over him.

I spent a lot of time on jobs with my dad especial-ly in summers; therefore I was exposed to Dink a lot.

After graduating high school I made my way to the working world in 1970 and started to work for a relative of ours, Nelson Lewis. He had bought the construction company that my dad and Dink had worked for years earlier. At first I was a truck driver, then on to an equipment operator before becoming a job foreman. This was all within the first year of my employment. After a short time, I was looking for more than just a wage, so I starting subcontracting from Nelson. Dink had a similar situation with Nelson.

One day Dink asked me if I thought it made sense for us to combine our efforts. He explained that there was always going to be slack periods from time to time and by pooling our workforces we would be more likely to weather those storms. I was able to see some logic in that so we shook hands and became partners. As it turned out our plan didn't work out all that well, so before too long we decided to pursue dreams without each other. Dink left Austin for greener pastures.

He drifted back through Austin occasionally, always calling me to meet up for coffee. Dink drank more coffee than any human being alive. I'm not sure he drank water very often and I never saw him drink alcohol. His personality was perfect to be a drunk, but early in his life he decided not to become one.

When we would meet there were always tall tales of mining for gold in Alaska, or diamonds in South Africa. He was living a life of adventure. He also built machines that would sink to the bottom of the sea floor and excavate soil and rocks, which would be operated remotely. He had a good mind for building contraptions.

In August of 73 Nelson and I formed Lewis Contractors, Inc; the company that is still operating today. By 1977 we had parted ways and I bought him out of that venture. Dink called me a couple of years later to ask if I would let him rent a piece of equipment on one of my accounts in Houston. He had contracted for some work and needed a little help. The mining days were behind him and it sounded like he was down on his luck. We had been friends for so long there was no way I could turn him down.

After three months the rentals had added up to just under $5,000 and I hadn't heard a word from Dink. I was headed down near Houston on other business with my accountant Woody Milsap along for the ride. He had been after me to collect the money from Dink, so I suggested that we try to find him. I didn't have a telephone number on him and only knew the general area where he was working. My luck was running pretty good that day. As I drove down Hwy. 1960, I looked over and there he was filling up with gas at an Exxon station. When I pulled up beside him, he said "Ron, so glad to see you. I was just filling up with gas so I could come to Austin and pay you the rent money on the backhoe."

Woody had never met Dink so I introduced them. Dink told us to pull around the corner and meet him at a doughnut shop for coffee. He said he would be there as soon as he finished filling his truck with gas and paid. Woody and I drank a cup of coffee. No Dink. Woody had heard all the wild stories about some of Dink and my misadventures, so he was already somewhat dubious of him. After a little while of sitting there, Woody said "Ron, I think your friend just cut out on us." I wasn't sure what to say. A few moments later Dink pulled up, walked in and handed me the check as he sat down. I slid the check in my pocket. We drank more coffee, listen to a few stories, laughed awhile, and then got back on the road.

We had traveled for a little while when Woody said "Ron, I notice you never looked at the check." I took the check out of my shirt pocket, looked at it and handed it to Woody. It appeared to both of us that not only was the check for the correct amount, but he had also signed it. What a guy I thought, that's the way friends should treat one another. I put the check back in my pocket, but a couple of

miles down the road it occurred to me that something wasn't right about that check. Taking the
check back out and giving it a closer examination I
discovered that the company name on the check was
Lewis Contractors. That was my company name. I
found out that Dink had established himself as Lewis Contractors, using accounts I had previously opened when doing work in Houston. He then had each
company send the bills to a new P.O. Box.

Dink returned the rental piece of equipment and
paid all the bills in full before leaving Houston to
pursue dreams elsewhere. Sometime later a banker
from the same bank that my check was drawn on called to tell me that an IRS agent was there wanting
the approximately $45,000 that Mr. McDuff had
left in an account. How he located me, I'll never
know. Dink must have listed me on that account also.
I told the banker that I had no interest in or connection to that money or Mr. McDuff.

I never heard another word from the banker, or
the IRS. Dink reappeared some months later. We
never discussed the Houston deal. What would have
been the point?

~~~~~~~~~~

Send His Long Tall Ass Back to Maarrble

As explained in an earlier story Dink and I became partners for a short period of time. We were sub-contracting under Nelson Lewis. During that time Nelson bought a set of 2-way radios. Not the Motorola brand. A knockoff that cost a fraction of what Motorola's cost. There were about 10 mobile units and a base station in the office. Dink and I each had one installed in our pickups. We decided that we often had business that neither Nelson, nor anyone else within the Nelson Lewis organization needed to hear.

So Dink made arrangements with Larry Byrd, the radio guru, to put an extra set of crystals in our two radios that would act as our own private channel when switched to the number 2 position on the dial. All we would had to do is say a special code word when we were on the main channel, then we would know to switch over for a private conversation. No one would ever even know about our secret channel. Dink was the first to get his radio up and running. Then later mine was ready for the big test run. After he knew I had mine "privatized," he gave me the special code word to switch over. This was going to be great. We talked along for a good while, as two guys would when they were just sitting around chatting.

The subject came up about something Nelson just might not completely agree on. Dink asked what I thought we should do if Nelson was going to resist us doing it our way. I said, "If he doesn't like it we'll just send his long tall ass back to Maarrble." I was referring to the town of Marble Falls, where Nelson resided.

A little while later, Dink called me and gave me the code to switch to channel 2. I complied. That is when Dink made me aware that he was talking on the base station radio in the office. Larry Byrd, the radio genius, had rigged the radios with a jumper wire that enabled everyone to hear, regardless of which channel we were on.

Nelson wasn't at the office, therefore probably didn't hear our chat, we reasoned. About lunch time Nelson called each of us and asked us to meet him for lunch. This was something we did several times each week. To our great relief he never said a word about the morning conversation. We had a very nice lunch. After paying the check and walking to the parking lot Nelson turned to us and said, "Well boys, I guess I better take my long tall ass back to Maarrble."

At that point he stepped into his car and drove off. The incident was never mentioned again. We promptly went to the radio shop to have those jumper wires removed.

~~~~~~~~~~

Dink - The Man - Part One

Dink was a-once-in-a-lifetime friend. He could do things to a friendship that would test it beyond limits. Yet I never went five minutes in his company without laughing. He was as much a comic entertainer as anyone you see now on TV or in the movies.

Like I said in another story Dink first entered my life when I was a preteen boy. He and my Dad worked construction together in the sixties. Although road boring is a dirty job typically mud and grease covers everything including the workers. Dinks trademark look was nice starched jeans and a white shirt. He always wore expensive cowboy boots made from exotic leathers. I think ostrich was his favorite. Of course various snakeskins were also in his closet or on his feet at times. He topped everything off with a big nice cowboy hat, always of the most expensive grade. He dressed that way every day. He'd jump right off into the bottom of an excavation with mud knee deep. When he came back to the surface he was cover from hat to boots with grease and mud. The next day he'd be right back dressed in his finest clothes, knowing what the day would hold for him.

Dink also wore lots of gold and diamonds. Few modern day pimps could out shine Dink in his day. Vehicles? No one drove fancier pickups than Dink. He would leave a dealership in a brand new truck, drive directly to a hot-rod shop to get loud pipes and fancy wheels put on it. This was before guys did that. We are talking the 60's and 70's.

Dink was a man of perhaps rugged good looks. Not to me, but to just about any waitress that ever walked up to his table. I never knew any man who drank more coffee and less alcohol who did construction. Most people that got to know him would have taken him to be a drunk. He had that appearance and manner about him. He smoked Pall Mall cigarettes without filters and he smoked a lot of them. You seldom saw him without a cigarette in his hand or mouth. He was small in stature, perhaps 5'7" and weighed in at 140 - max.

Dink was a good 20 years older than me. I had known Dink in the mid 60's but when 1972 rolled around I was an adult and got to know him on a different level. We became friends and spent a lot of time together. According to my wife, we spent way

too much time together. We had only been married
for a short time then. Dink and I met for coffee
early each morning, we'd have lunch together and
most of the time meet up for coffee a couple of
times in the afternoon. I can see where she may
have thought we were spending too much time together.

I'll never forget Dink had a friend he'd met in the
coffee shop who had a business supply store. So he
decided to get us each business cards made. When
he went to pick them up a few days later he proudly
he handed me both boxes so I could have a few of
his and him a few of mine. I opened his box to find
that his name 'Dink' had become 'Pink'. I was kidding
him about just using them anyway when he open mine
and said, "Ok 'Rinnie', let's just do that." Needless to
say we were delayed a few days getting our business
cards handed out.

A most memorable time was when we went to meet
a man originally from Smithwick who I'd know my
whole life. Duff McClish was a heck of a good guy
and your very personable insurance salesman type.
On our way to meet him, Dink McDuff got me to repeat his name once more. The wheels were turning.
Duff stood up as we approached his table and stuck
his hand out and said, "I'm Duff McClish..." and Dink,

without missing a beat said, "I'm pleased to meet you I'm Clish McDuff."

I'm not sure you can get the true effect of us sitting down and after a few minutes Duff said, "Tell me again what your name is?" To which Dink replied, "My name is George McDuff, but everyone just calls me Clish." That was the humor of Dink McDuff.

After our business venture fell apart he went on to pursue many other interests. He always had something interesting going on. He came to town one day and called so we could meet up. He was dating a real young gal from Louisiana. Her father and Dink were almost identically the same age. His name was Bob. I met him once and thought they even favored. Bob worked for the Coast Guard and was pretty high up. He and Dink designed this apparatus so when a ship or a barge rammed, or got rammed, it was like a large diaper with a cable harness that would cover a hole, or split, and the outside would inflate forming a seal against the hub. This would stop the leak until the oil, or other liquid could be pumped off.

He had a small prototype built. It really was impressive. They had started the patent process and if I gave him a certain amount of money I could have a certain stake in this thing. He had made a deal with this patent attorney that he would walk the whole thing through and do everything for $12,000 cash.

When Dink had a deal for you it was never anything like you had ever heard before. It wasn't, "You give me $12,000 and next year when this thing is going it will be worth $24,000." No it was... "Give me $12,000 and next year alone our profits will reach 46 million and you'll get 20% of that!" He and Bob would each have 40%.

How was this going to work? "Several vessels in Louisiana had recently ruptured creating an environmental disaster and the Coast Guard would require every type of floating anything to carry one of these diaper kits on board. If they were allowed in US waters they would have to be equipped with this safety device." Dink left Austin with $12,000 cash. My cash. I'll have to continue this when my eyes can focus.

~~~~~~~~~~

Dink - The Man – Part Two

After Dink left with the money I didn't hear from him. Not for about 2 years. Probably the longest that I'd not heard from him in my adult life. It's pretty easy to figure when someone is dodging you.

We had some common acquaintances so I'd have some idea what he was up to and eventually found out he was up in Irving Texas area.

Since my $9 million royalty check never arrived for the boat diaper and Madeline and I needed to get away for the weekend, Irving seemed like a good way to head. I knew he hung out at a certain Denny's in Irving, so we went there first. I cornered the manager and after visiting a few minutes found out he hadn't been around for a couple of months. But he had moved up to McKinney and bought a little farm. We headed to McKinney.

As we drove along I-75 north out of Dallas, Madeline and I talked about how unlikely it was we would actually find Dink. Going along we passed a Holiday Inn on the right and I said, "That's where Dink drinks coffee several times a day... since it's getting late let's go back there and get a room for the night." That way we could head back home in the morning. We walked in and as we waited at the check-in counter, I just asked the hostess of the restaurant, who was standing nearby, "Has Dink been in today?" She said, "He was here this morning and he should be here anytime now, he sits with that table of guys." At the table were several rancher types that looked like they came there every day before going out to feed last thing in the afternoon.

I got Madeline around to the room and walked back to the restaurant taking a seat at a table facing the only seat left at the table of guys. Dink walked in moments later and sat down. You could tell that they were waiting for him to come in to tell them stories and make them laugh. He looked over and saw me. If he was surprised he didn't really show it. He came over and joined me. He explained how when he left Austin that day and went to see the patent attorney in Houston his truck, the prototype, and his brief case with the money, and all the paperwork had been stolen. He just couldn't bear the thought of telling me. So he dodged me for a couple years. One more dream of his was down the drain.

~~~~~~~~~~~

Dink - The Final Chapter

While there are many more Dink stories I'll skip ahead for Dink's final salvo. Dink could and did extract money from me on several occasions. He had a good deal for me almost every time I saw him. He wanted to see me become rich right along with him. He never did become rich. He didn't do much for my bottom line either, at least positively. Dink always was a lady's man; a real charmer. He charmed me often, but with time we lost touch. By happen-stance I ran onto him in a café in north Texas one day in 1991. We visited. He had a deal for me, but I wasn't interested.

My life became busy and with our history it was easy enough for me to not worry about Dink. But for some reason one day in the fall of 2003, while driving to Dallas, I started thinking about him. Since the internet came along I had honed my skills in the art of finding people. Skip tracing became a real hobby. Within a few minutes I had located him. He was living in Irving. I could tell he was living at the same address as several females. Had Dink finally set up a situation to where he had his own harem?

Upon closer examination I discovered the ladies were old. Really old. It was a nursing home. I think he was 70 by that time. I drove there that day. When I walked in he was sitting in a chair, he looked up and said, "Damn Ron, I was wondering when you'd show up." He had spent most his life smoking cigarettes without a filter. Several pack a day. Almost more than anyone I knew. His lungs were pretty well shot. He was pitiful in one way, but still had the ability to tell a good story. A lady he had met in their respective favorite coffee shop came regularly to be sure he had what he needed. There was no family close by. Without his friend I'm sure he wouldn't have lasted nearly as long. He had the means to still have a cell phone so we swapped numbers and talked often. I would get to Dallas every few months and go see him. I gave him a $100 bill each time I left.

In 2005 I received a call from his friend, saying he had died. Dink had another friend who was a land developer in DFW; Bill I think his name was. I met him once. When Dink's time was getting short he was ask by his lady friend what to do about paying for his funeral. He said, "Get ahold of Bill and Ronnie and they'll take care of it."

When I got to the Funeral Home in east Texas, I paid my half and I suppose Bill did the same. Afterwards I met with some of his family members from west Texas at a Luby's and had lunch. We swapped Dink stories. I told them about the funeral arrangements that Dink had made. I said, "I gladly paid it, figuring that would be the last time he'd be able to get in my pocket." We all laughed. They knew Dink too.

~~~~~~~~~~

It Sat There All Day

When Kenny had a ranch in Mexico and was going back and forth a lot he bought a helicopter. He also used it to look at projects around the state. It was pretty handy. I had a lease agreement with him, so when I'd need to get around taking care of business it was at my disposal. To make sure I was as cool as my brother I built a helipad at my house. The pilot would fly in, grab me and we could leave Bertram and be in Arlington, Tx in an hour and twenty minutes.

One day about 3 years ago he was flying me up to Lubbock to look at a project we were bidding. It was early morning. I ran over to the store to grab something while I waited on my ride. I had quite a bit of stuff I was carrying along so when I got back I pulled up close to the pad. In a short while he landed and we took off headed to Lubbock. Late that afternoon Madeline called me to see if there was a reason for my Suburban to be sitting at the helipad with the engine running? Son Mike happened to come by and noticed it. I had pulled up and left it running that morning. Even more amazing, it had been running, still in drive, for about 10 hours.

~~~~~~~~~~

Kenny's Present to Me

Kenny went off to an auction one Saturday where wildlife and birds of all sorts were being sold. This was at the very end of the big Ostrich craze. You know what I mean. There have been several others too, the Emu, the Llama, the Alpaca where anybody that's anybody has to have some if they ever expect to become wealthy.

Anyway Ken decided my little estate could use a couple of the giant birds. So unbeknownst to me he pulled in and opened the trailer gate and made me the proud owner of the two beasts. Like I said the craze had passed so the once $10,000 birds were worth about nothing. But with plenty of room for them to roam I thought they were a pretty good novelty item to have around. Several of the boys were still living at home and with friends often coming over, they would occasionally run them down and swing on for a ride.

One day Chuck, the top cop here in our little town, (he was the only cop) stopped by. He had a problem. A woman with a kid about 10 or 11 in tow showed up at the police station homeless. Bertram may have problems but homelessness isn't one of them, so he didn't know what to do. He thought maybe I could figure out a place they could stay until other arrangements could be made.

We cleaned out a corner of my shop building and put a couple of cots back there for them to sleep on. Not exactly living in the lap of luxury, but better than sleeping on a park bench. Being just a short distance from town, they could walk there for food. I gave them a small pittance so they could do just that.

The next afternoon when I got home there was a trail of blood leading across the driveway right in through the garage and into the kitchen. Ron Jr. had every medical supply in the house out on the kitchen table and he and the woman were trying to bandage the kids badly cut foot. He had been messing around out in his new home and picked up a big mirror that was stored there; he dropped it, broke it and sliced his foot. Finally with it cleaned, doctored, and taped up we got them out of the house, (Our House) and back out in their new home.

With disaster averted, I went off to work the next morning. When I came in that afternoon, Ron Jr had them back in the kitchen bandaging up the woman's wounds she received when she, walking across the pasture from town, was attacked by one of ostriches. The woman was cut, scraped and bruised all over.

None of us know for sure but it's thought that as they were walking the big birds came up and scared them... the woman took off running and her feet got tangled up, she tripped and fell and maybe repeated that several more times. Because the feathered creatures had never actually flogged anyone else we didn't buy that they suddenly began attacking previously homeless people out for a walk.

Deciding that things weren't going to get any better, I had Ron Jr load up our guest and take them to Austin. All I could think of was the next thing I knew the woman and the kid would be living in the big house with Madeline, the boys and me living in the corner of the shop. That brought an end to the Bertram homeless problem and we got to keep our home.

That didn't end the ostrich story. We drove out in the pasture one day and one of them was walking around with its head down almost dragging the ground. Strangest thing I had seen in a while. I secretly wondered if one of the boys had broken its neck swinging up on it to take a joy ride. By the next day big bird was dead. The one single goofy looking fowl continued to walk around in circles all day long, maybe looking for its friend, but finally went back to walking around eating grasshoppers and other stuff.

When the twins got old enough to drive we went off to south Austin to buy them some transportation. We found a couple of little pickups. One was a black Mazda and the other a gray Ford Ranger. They were not very old and fairly low miles so we figured they would last through high school for them.

Teenage boys first getting used to driving don't always put pickups in gear, or set the parking brakes. Justin, the black Mazda driver, was the guilty one. When we got home we noticed the pickup sitting down in the pasture. I thought... being new to vehicle ownership why would he just get out and leave it down there like that?

When I walked in the house and saw him sitting there I asked him why his new truck was way down in the pasture. You could tell by the look on his face that he was completely unaware. The pickup had rolled down the gravel road and exited the fenced-in area around the house by rolling squarely across the cattle guard toward a stock tank that was a couple of hundred yards further down. It had stopped a ways short of the water.

When we reached the truck it appeared everything was fine. It had just been left in neutral. Not a scratch on it. Lucky us. Justin, in his haste, had forgotten the keys so he returned to the house to get them. At the same time as he started back down to retrieve his little pickup, from across the pasture the lone ostrich came at a full run. Without even slowing down the damn thing crashed into the front fender of the truck, fell down, got back up and kept charging the door and side of the black truck until there wasn't a straight piece of metal on the left side.

Justin finally was able to get in and drive safely across the fence before the darn thing completely totaled out the truck. Immediately a contract was put out on the life of the one ostrich. The only condition was it had to be a clean shot to the head. It was carried out swiftly.

Note to the Folks from the ASPCA.... there is a ten year statute of limitation on cruelty to animal charges and it's been 16 years.

~~~~~~~~~~

Kenny Found Himself in a Tight Squeeze

Work was slow for us in the construction business. We decided that the one of utility trailers could use a new floor. David, my brother in law, was selected for that task.

We used oak lumber and it had to have a hole drilled for each bolt that attached it to the trailer. David was using a 3/4" electric drill. It was powerful and sometimes hard to keep a hold of. David was always a little jumpy, especially if someone touched his rear end. As he struggled with the job at hand, Kenny walked up behind him and stuck the toe of his boot up and touched his privates.

Just then David swung around holding the drill with the trigger locked on and made a jab at Kenny. As Kenny turned to run, he was about one step too slow. The drill bit caught him right in the seat of his jeans. That's when the excitement really began. The drill was jerked out of David's hands. As he ran the drill and Kenny became one. Luckily for him, there was only about 50 feet of extension cord stretched out. When he reached the end of the cord it unplugged.

That drill had twisted so tight that the entire seat of his Wrangler jeans was torn out. That's not to even mention his own condition. A good laugh was had by all. Well... maybe all except Kenny. Even he was able to laugh about it later, after the blood blister went away and swelling went down.

~~~~~~~~~~

It Wasn't Me

Kenny has always had a lot of company pride. He likes all of his machines looking good and clean.

Everything needs to be ship-shape in Kenny Lewis's world. He enjoys having his company name on jackets and caps. He spends a lot of advertising bucks and it pays off for him. I see people wearing them often, putting the CCI logo out in public.

Kenny and I had an arrangement for about a decade that lasted until 2003. We pooled resources and CCI was the name that was in the forefront of the business. Advertising was good so all of his people and all of my people wore CCI labeled caps and jackets. When times changed and we decided both of our situations would be better to part ways, we carefully planned how to re-brand the companies and make a smooth transition.

There were a few boxes of leftover caps sitting in my office. One day a couple of my guys got a box each of the caps and started handing them out to the homeless people around Austin. If you have ever been around Austin you know that panhandling is only second in number of people to state workers.

Within days everywhere you went in Austin a guy or gal was sporting a red CCI cap. Seemed like pretty good exposure to me. Not that I had anything to do with them handing out the caps, please understand. But when Kenny drove through the city and saw all those caps, my phone started ringing. "You think you're pretty damn funny don't you Ronnie Gene Lewis!" Of course not knowing anything about what he was referring to, I said, "Ken, what's going on?" "You know &@$%#^*^#}¥€>‹€*%+, well what I'm talking about." I chuckled inside. Not that I had anything to do with it, please understand.

He was truly ticked off, only like Kenny Lewis can be ticked off. He didn't like that kind of exposure. My denials fell on deaf ears. He was convinced I was behind it. But please understand I had nothing to do with it. I told him so. I think he hung up on me a time or two. "Calm down Kenny, can't you just go around town with a pocket full of tens, and buy them back?" was my suggestion. That wasn't what he wanted to hear.

I finally figured shutting up would serve me best for a while. He called me a day or two later explaining what his plan for retaliation was. He was going to order a few boxes of black Lewis Contractors caps and go around and swap them for his red caps. "Fine with me, I would like people in Austin to know I'm willing to help the homeless population!" was my response. I even sent the LC logo over so he would have a leg up on getting the caps made.

I guess he thought better of his idea, because I never saw any of my caps on Austin street corners.

The red ones started disappearing and soon there wasn't one in site. Rumor was a few of them were forcibly taken from bums around town but I have no proof of it.

~~~~~~~~~~

The Fruit Basket

Growing up in Smithwick you knew everyone who ever came through the place. After getting out of school and marrying, I left for Austin and would get back up there every few weeks. But things were changing faster than I could keep up.

The 225 acres that Kenny and I grew up on was being sold off in small tracts. While it's no secret we didn't really like that Cec was selling it, it wasn't our choice. He had inherited the property in 1958 when his Dad, our Grandfather Theron, passed away. But it appeared that selling off the place was going to give Cecil and Bonnie Gay some measure of comfort and the lake property would remain in the family along with some other property. It would have been a little too self-serving for us to have said much about it.

Some 20 years later Bonnie Gay died and then Cec did the same 5 years later. The landscape and demographic had changed a lot over the course of the 25 years. We knew some of the people he had sold to, while others we got to know over time.

The third component in the demographic was people who had moved in that we didn't know and for the most part didn't want to know. As long as Cec was alive there wasn't a big need for a Property Owners Association, he pretty well just made sure most routine stuff a POA is for got done.

Now it was a pretty sure bet that Kenny and I were not going to be babysitting the place as Cec had done, so a POA was established. We felt good about it and willing to do what we could to help out. But the fly in the ointment was this one Yankee acting SOB, (who must not have been filled in on the history of the situation) was voted in as president. I'm not certain whether this was immediately, or whether he came along a few years into the POA.

To get to the property that we still owned along the lake we drove the same road as the property owners did to get to the land that was designated as the POA Park. From the road everything to the left was the property owner's park and everything on the right of the road belonged to Kenny and me.

This Yankee, (there may have been others as well) I'll just call him Bill for this purpose; decided they didn't want people going and coming to the park without going through a gate first. What Bill and the others may not have taken into full consideration was that the road along the POA Park was actually on property that belonged to Kenny and me. A nice new gate was erected right at the beginning of the park, part way down a hill.

Kenny kept livestock on our lake property and we all used it for recreation. Kenny being the one who was in and out regularly and also the one that was going to be inconvenienced the most (and was the least likely to put up with any horseshit from anyone) stopped and told the fellow we are calling Bill to take that damn gate out and don't be long about it.

I'm not sure if Bill was hard of hearing or stupid, perhaps both, but he didn't heed the warning Kenny Lewis had given him. From that point on when Kenny came off the hill, if the gate was shut he would plow through it with the big Ranch Hand Grill Guard on his handsomely decked out pickup. As time went on pieces of the gates were lying all over the area.

It took a little while for it to sink in on Old Bill that he was going to eat up the entire budget of the POA, just buying gates. Eventually the gate issue was pretty much resolved. Bill lived just about a hundred yards from the entry to the park, so he vowed to keep an eye on things and keep people out that weren't supposed to be in the park. Great idea I guess.

A few years later our son Justin was going with a little gal over in Burnet. Let's call her Lauren. Her family was having a get together and she asked if they could use our lovely place down at the lake. I told her to just go on down there and make it their own for the weekend. On Friday she and her grandmother went to scope out the place and to see what all they would need to make it an enjoyable outing. Lauren had a brand spankin new Ford Mustang her folks had just bought her. Well when they had looked around and headed out Bill stopped them. He went up one side and down the other about what their intentions were and this, that and the other.

Scared the young lady and the older woman half to death. When Lauren came over to the house that evening she asked me if I was sure it was going to be alright for them to go down to the lake the next day. She went on to tell me about the encounter with Bill.

Whether you know me very well or not I bet you can imagine how that news was received. In about 15 seconds I had Bill on the phone explaining a few facts of life to him. Out of respect for Lauren and my family members I finally walked outside with a remote phone to my ear. Not that I really needed it, as he's only about 15 miles across the way as the crow flies. I'm sure he could hear me clearly in that short distance. "YOU MORON DO YOU THINK A YOUNG GIRL AND OLD LADY IN A NEW MUSTANG FITS THE DESCRIPTION OF PEOPLE GOING IN DO-ING DAMAGE TO THE PARK PROPERTY - IN THE MIDDLE OF THE DAY?"

After I calmed down enough for him to speak, he asks how he could make up for the wrong he had caused. I said, "Get your ass up to town in the morn-ing and you have two choices. You get the most beau-tiful bouquet of flowers you can find, or get a nice fruit basket and a big one at that, when you see all those people have arrived take that gift down there and give it to the two ladies you offended. But I don't want you lingering, after you do that, get your butt back up to your house and stay out of sight the rest of the day! If you don't do exactly like in telling you, I'll be over there stomping a mud hole in your ass."

He chose the fruit basket. A beautiful fruit basket. I think he must have gotten his very sweet wife (I've been told she is) to help him really make it look nice. Lauren took a picture of it. That man sure has been neighborly since then. I never seen or heard another thing from him since that time. But it has only been 12 or 14 years.

~~~~~~~~~~

The Hitchhiker

One evening, several years ago, Kenny stopped by my place in Bertram. He had a lot to say, but I don't remember him saying anything that enlightened me much that night. That happens sometimes when he has made a trip or two too many to the cooler in the back of his pickup; at least back at that point in time. He was living on out the road from me about 5 or 6 miles. As the night wore on and I wore down I suggested that the best idea was for him to come in and make the couch his bed for the night. We had been sitting out in his pickup, on his pickup, or where ever felt best for that particular hour.

With my offer of a place to lay down rejected, he left for the midnight drive down the dark desolate road to his humble abode. With Madeline and all the boys tucked comfortably in bed for what had been hours at that time, I carefully tip-toed through the house being sure not to turn on a light or slam a door. I eased into bed and laid there with the night's conversation churning in my head.

After a little while I heard sirens from town. They came our way and continued on out the road. Since few cars ever traveled out that road late at night I knew what the possibilities were. After a bit I got up, dressed and hit the road north. A mile or 2 short of Kenny's place was his pickup setting up on top of the bridge railing at the North San Gabriel River where it goes under FM 1174. Lots of flashing lights and road flares werealready set out. Kenny was fine, standing there talking to several of Burnet Counties finest.

As I moved in closer I heard him telling them how this horrible situation came about. He had drank too much at my house and realizing he had no business driving when he got to the end of my driveway had pulled over to sleep it off. Just then he heard a tap on his window and rolled it down. Evidently, the fellow had been stranded in town and needed to get about 7 miles out into the country. Coincidently his destination was very near to where Kenny lived. Kenny then told the officers that the guy didn't seem to be impaired so, as a benefit to them both, a deal was struck to where Kenny would be driven home, and then the fellow could easily make it on foot to his destination.

The only unfortunate thing about the arrangement was that the guy took his eyes off the road. The pickup first went up on the guardrail, clipping the domed topped wooden posts off like they were tooth picks (there was creosote wood all up and down the highway) until it reached the concrete barrier wall and continue until the friction ground the wild ride to a halt. Kenny had even asked his driver to slow-down, but the guy ignored him. Then after totaling Kenny's pickup, the guy jump out and started running down the river into the darkness.

The cops were standing there shaking their heads at the whole story when Kenny blurted out the best line of the night... "Why are y'all just standing here when you could be down that creek apprehending the guy that caused this whole mess? Can't you call for a helicopter to help search for him?" To this day the hitchhiker has never been caught, nor has he turned himself in.

~~~~~~~~~~~

Santa Comes to Dripping Springs

We had moved to Dripping Springs in the mid 80's. It was a great place to raise kids. Life was really wonderful. Madeline was able to find something to occupy her time with every second of every day. And night. All of the little angels were involved in sports and a variety of other activities. We had an active church life with a great church family.

Madeline was the Den Mother for the younger boys. It was Christmas time and we were hosting a party out at our place. Bunches of little Cub Scouts were everywhere. Madeline could talk my brother Kenny into doing anything. Santa parked his pickup up at the highway and made the 300 yard walk down the little gravel lane to the Lewis house. With a big Ho Ho Ho, the jolly man arrived with a sack full of toys over his shoulder. It was all just perfect. The best Santa ever.

With Ron Jr. standing beside me, I pointed out to him that something a little fishy was going on. (Ron was about 10 or 11 at that time I think) Santa had on a pair of cowboy boots. Pulling Ron aside, I suggested that in a few minutes as Santa exited, let him get to the gate then he, Ron, could rally the little cubbies to all chase after Santa and see how fast he could run in those boots.

Just as planned, when Santa had a good 50 yard head start, Ron, the twins, and a whole passel of young scouts began running after him, pelting him with rocks. It was about the funniest Santa departure you could ever imagine.

Shortly afterwards Santa, now dressed as Kenny, showed up to enjoy an afternoon of partying with us.

~~~~~~~~~~

The Bank Depositor

One day in the 80's Kenny was driving and I was the passenger. That's generally the way we have always traveled. Who needs to listen to a bunch of belly-aching about my driving? Not me.

So, since I didn't have to watch the road and see what he was about the crash into, I decided to read the newspaper. There was a story that I found intriguing. It was about this new bank they were opening in Austin and they were only going to have women customers.

Relating the story to Kenny got him all stirred up. "This Women's Lib crap, with equal rights has just about gone far enough!" Then he went on with, "What do you think they'd be saying if men opened a bank that excluded women?"

Seeing that he was getting a little too worked up I decided to explain that it wasn't a regular bank. It was a bank for mother's breast milk.

We made the rest of the trip without him even so much as looking over at me

~~~~~~~~~~

A Typical, Yet Untypical Vacation

One of our family vacations that we were able to plan ahead and actually take was to California. I say that, because many times we planned vacations and because of being self-employed the business would get shoved in front of family. For that I'm regretful but being in business afforded us opportunities that perhaps we wouldn't have had otherwise.

This year, 1986 I think it was, took us to Los Angeles to do some of the same things most people do when there. Universal Studios and other Hollywood stuff, went to see the RMS Queen Mary in Long Beach, as well as the Spruce Goose, Howard Hughes mammoth plane made from plywood.

When we first headed out I was having severe back and leg pain. Not long before I had been through surgery for a ruptured disk in my neck. It seemed that the craziness of my childhood antics was catching up with me. We had a rented minivan so here we were all 7 packed into it running around southern California. We then headed out to Hesperia, Ca. to see my Aunt Cokie and Uncle Gene for a couple of days. They showed us around that area. I kept eating pain pills and making the most of the vacation.

Next we planned to go back to LA, spend the night and board a train to travel along the coastline up to San Francisco. There we had a motorhome reserved and planned to do the SF tourist stuff then head over to Yosemite for a few days before flying   back home.

On Sunday afternoon, trying to make our way to a hotel close to the LA Train Station from Hesperia, we had a blowout on the minivan. In typical California Highway Patrol fashion an officer was there within minutes to be sure we were safe. I was able to get far enough off the road onto the media to be safe but the officer remained with us. We called to get the rental company to come change the tire. (I'm sorry to say I looked in the manual and still couldn't find the spare tire or jack.) Besides we were paying good money and I wanted service and my leg hurt.

He inquired as to where we were from. I proudly said Texas. When he ask where we were headed, for some stupid reason, instead of saying the train station, I said LAX. I inferred that I hoped we could get there before we missed our flight. I think it was the pain pills talking, but I reasoned that as nice and helpful as he was, maybe he would load all 7 of us, along with all our suitcases in his patrol car and drive us completely across LA so we wouldn't miss our flight. I know it was the pills talking because it was very irrational thinking on my part.

The cop then looked at me and said something I don't think I'll ever forget. "Only an idiot Texan would come to California and decide to drive all the way across Los Angeles on a Sunday evening when you could have just taken a flight out of this airport right here..." Pointing to the Ontario Airport - to which we were sitting directly in front of.

My lie was already out and it wasn't like I wanted to recant and start over admitting we were actually going to the train station and not the airport. So I blurted out, "That's what I get for leaving all the travel arrangements up to my wife." Then I realized Madeline was sitting there with her window open listening to the whole conversation from start to finish. I could tell she wasn't happy. When she finally got me out of earshot of the policeman she started in on me: "Why did you tell him.................?" It was unexplainable by me.

The cop, knowing that he had me on the ropes, in very California sarcastic style; he decided to toss one insult after another my way. I couldn't say anything for fear that I'd just dig myself in deeper. That's when I took to keeping my distance from him. When he'd head to my side of the car, I'd ease the other way. If I was in the front and he'd head that way, I'd head to the back, as if trying to find something I had lost. Luckily the rental company guy showed up about the same time as a relief cop came. It was shift change time. I was happy to see the insulter go on his merry way. It was during that time waiting and dodging the cop that I made a promise to myself. I would never ever tell another lie, no matter how harmless it may seem.

With the tire changed we continued on to our hotel, where I dropped Madeline and the boys and then took the car on to LAX for a drop off. (See I hadn't actually lied after all) I knew there wouldn't be time the next morning. Finally getting back by taxi, it was time for bed.

We boarded the train early the next morning. It was probably the prettiest sites I could have ever imagined as we made the train trip north. I'm not sure I ever even look out all day. My leg hurt that bad. When we made it to San Francisco late that day, we talked about the need to pull the plug on the motorhome trip to Yosemite. Instead we'd just rent another minivan and settle for staying in the San Francisco area for the duration.

We checked into our rooms (we always had to get 2 rooms) and went to sleep. The next morning I told Madeline I would just stay behind and try to get my leg feeling better. The wheels were churning in my head. They stayed out all day long. By the time they returned to the hotel to read my note, I was already back in Texas and stretched out on my own bed in Dripping Springs.

She wasn't very happy with me. But I knew if I told her my plan she would insist on the whole family cutting things short and heading home. I didn't think that was fair and she was very capable of handling things without me. They finished the trip and brought home many good memories.

~~~~~~~~~~

The Sailfish

Madeline and I had traveled to Acapulco, Mexico for a getaway in the late 70's. It was enjoyable and we wanted to go back. So we convinced my parents to go with us.

Wanting to make the most of the trip and do something memorable for them, we lined up a parasailing ride for Bonnie Gay. She was extremely proud that she had tried it. Madeline took pictures, but then discovered the film wasn't loaded correctly. So she gladly went for a second round. The pictures turned out good.

Cec didn't try it, but when he got back home he went directly to the Army Surplus store in Lampasses and bought a parachute. It was just a regular one - not made for parasailing. There is a difference. With a regular old parachute, if you were lucky enough to get it airborne, it almost assuredly would get up to a pretty good height then dive bomb into the water below.

Poor ole Virgil Lackey, a Smithwick resident back in those days, could attest to it not being a safe practice to let Cecil Lewis strap you in a parachute and take off pulling you. I never witnessed it in action, thank heavens. By the time I showed back up to the lake, the parasailing Smithwick style was but a painful memory.

There were several other memorable times on that trip although Cec didn't travel so well. Sometimes he was known to overindulge in drink if he was off and supposed to be having a good time. The highlight of the trip was a deep sea fishing charter to catch sailfish.

As we prepared to head out that morning, we went to get box lunches. I have a total phobia about eating in Mexico, from a trip made there soon after Madeline and I married (which is a whole other story.) Knowing what my limitations were on eating we found a Colonel Sanders Kentucky Fried Chicken on our way to the docks. Figuring if the Colonel fixed it I wouldn't end up with dysentery so we went with KFC.

It wasn't an experience like I'd ever had fishing off the coast of Texas. The boat was old and very antiquated. We got far enough out to catch a big sailfish but could still see land. The crew was sizable. There was the Captain and crew of about six, and the four of us.

We didn't find an elusive sailfish for a while; then something big hit one of the lines. They finally brought a very large turtle on board then stuck it up in the front of the boat. Later the boat came to a stop and we were told it was time to eat. As we began to eat our chicken, they brought the turtle out near where we were. With a large knife they cut its throat and bled it out into a couple of big plastic cup. All of the crew then started passing the cups from one to the other, consuming the warm thick blood. I did my own brand of chumming over the side of the boat. I feel sure if the others in our party of four didn't, they weren't far from it.

With lunch over with, the trolling resumed. Almost instantly Bonnie Gay and I both hooked up at the same time. Mine was made easy as the line was wrapped around its tail and it mostly laid there as I powered winched it in. Bonnie Gay's fought and she stayed with it. I'm not sure how long it took for her to land it, but she enjoyed every minute of it.

Once we were back to the dock there was a frenzy of men wanting to be the one that got our business to taxidermy our two fish. Finally one fellow prevailed and a deal was struck. I gave him about $600 dollars and we swapped information.

Over the next few months I made many phone calls trying to find out about the fish. I had misunderstood; he would need more money to finish the work. I almost called a halt to it, but decided that my mother was so thrilled about her catch, that I didn't want to disappoint her so I telegraphed the additional funds. Next I got a notice from the guy saying the fish were ready to ship.

But he needed more money to crate and ship them. Once again I had misunderstood. So I sent more money. A few days later I got a call from Continental Airlines that I had 2 large packages at the Austin Airport ready to be picked up. I had waited so long and paid so much I hurried out to get them.

I got to the airport to find out the shipment has been sent COD. More money was required to get the fish. Knowing this was the end of it. I gladly paid the money and took the two big crates back to the office so we could finally see the finished master-pieces. They looked good, but then I discovered that it was just 2 big chunks of plaster of Paris with the fin being cut from a piece of Masonite then all paint-ed up. The only thing that could have been from the fish was the long bill, but now I even question that. In all the two stuffed fish cost me around $2000. That was a lot of money in 1980.

Bonnie Gay proudly displayed her fish in her home. I think my trophy may have stayed crated. I didn't need to have it on constant display to remind me of the chump I'd been.

~~~~~~~~~~

The Thoughtfulness of My Brother

One day my brother Kenny walked into my woodshop carrying a wooden saddle rack that he had bought somewhere. He asked if I could carve a name and maybe put something fancy on it. The rack was fairly simple, made from pine, just plain looking.

He told me the story of seeing a saddle in the barn of an old cowboy friend of his. He asked about the saddle and got a complete history of it. The old cowboy had owned that saddle most of his adult life I believe. He told Kenny who made it and what it cost. He had sat a straddle of it for many many years. Now, as the years had caught up to him, the saddle was just left hanging there in the barn. Kenny told him he sure did like the saddle. I'm not sure but maybe after a few visits and talks about the saddle, the old cowboy gave it to him.

Kenny took it to a fine saddle repair shop and had it completely reconditioned. He wanted the rack to display the saddle on. It seemed like a good story so I asked if I could make a special rack for that special saddle. He said for me to get with it.

I had some wonderful red cedar lumber, so using the other rack as a pattern I went to work. I had never built one before but I just copied the other one. I carved the old cowboys name and where he had spent his whole life ranching on one end; a cattle drive scene on the other end.

When it was all finished I called Kenny to come pick it up. When we strapped the saddle on the rack it was a magnificent sight. Later that afternoon he took it back to the old cowboy and carried it into his living room where it has remained ever since.

~~~~~

D.L. "Punk" Turner, you are one of the two finest, most honest men to ever sit in a saddle. The other being your brother, G.H. "Son" Turner.

~~~~~

A FEW LAST WORDS FROM THE AUTHOR

I just realized that perhaps telling the stories of my life are much like my life has been, fast and furious. Dang, I shouldn't use the phrase 'Fast and Furious' because that term has taken on the meaning of something screwed up, out of control, just plain crazy. On second thought I guess it does apply to my life since I have spent a lifetime randomly telling tales of what it is like being Ronnie Lewis.

Like so many things, pacing yourself is the best way to go through life, but I've always thought I would be a better short distance runner than a marathoner. If I am going to run a race I just need to get started and finished just as fast as possible. Twenty six miles takes too long to run. I'm like the little boy that plays so hard he forgets to stop and pee.

A few weeks ago yesterday, I was standing in line at Luby's at noon. Rather than being bored I had my iPhone in my hand fiddling with it and created *The Angora Chronicles* on Facebook before I passed the salads. A week later I had told perhaps half the stories I know.

Funny how it works though, every time I tell a story three more pop into my mind. Does that mean that I'll never stop thinking of something else to say? Most likely not, but they just may not be as amusing.

But who knows... I still live in a world full of crazy things going on around us. So maybe things will keep on happening until Madeline falls across my casket and cry's out, "Oh why did it have to be this One!"

I've been told I never know when to shut up. I start talking and before I know what's happened, everyone around me knows more about me than I do...

So... Stay Tuned For MORE

For More Now check out The Angora Chronicles on Facebook... Leave a Comment... Share Your Own Stories...

~~~~~~~~~~~

Ronnie Lewis

Made in the USA
Columbia, SC
22 November 2020